What people are saying about

Entrusting the Key

"Bold, fresh, vibrant! Ali Smith unfolds a story of love, growth, and good choices in a way every reader will take home golden nuggets of hope and help."

Pam Farrel
Author, over 30 books including best selling
Men are like Waffles, Women are like Spaghetti

"In these pages, Ali Smith articulates her exploration of singleness with remarkable authenticity and her trademark passion…
you can find the intimacy with God she's found along the way.
It will change everything."

Susan D. Hill
Author, *Closer Than Your Skin: Unwrapping the Mystery of Intimacy with God*

"This book is a must-read especially for young adults who are searching for God's will for their life and relationships. Ali shares candidly about her personal journey with God, including the roller-coaster ride of emotions that all of us face. Her journey is your journey; I believe her discovery will become your discovery. You will want to share this with others too."

The Rev. Dr. Naomi Dowdy
President, Naomi Dowdy Ministries
Resident Apostle, Trinity Christian Centre, Singapore

"Ali Smith takes readers on her delightful journey to find the love of her life. That journey hasn't finished yet, but Ali discovers along the way that life's greatest "romance" is a vital, daily relationship with the Lord. Considering that choice of spouse is life's most important decision after a personal commitment to Christ, Ali's book is a must-read for anyone seeking God's direction in finding a life mate."

John Maust
President, Media Associates International, USA

"As I read…I couldn't help thinking how much I hope my own daughters are surrounded by women like Ali Smith, who combine a great joy of life with a desire to hear the voice of our God. I admire Ali's desire to please God as well as acknowledging the complexity of growing into maturity with all its' conflicting demands. I encourage you to walk alongside Ali, and see the power of God working through her life."

The Rev. John Crosby
Board Member , World Vision
Head Pastor, Christ Presbyterian Church of Edina, Minnesota, USA

"God gives each of His children opportunities to trust Him in life situations they encounter. With humor and honesty, Ali Smith recounts the ups and downs of her journey as a single woman while learning more about God's love and care for her. While the experiences recounted in this book are uniquely Ali's, the deep longings of her heart are universal.
As I have spent time with single women on four continents,
I have observed that God often uses matters of the heart to sift and reveal the true level of one's relationship with God and calls young women, like Ali, to trust Him - even when it is not easy."

Jeannette Shubert, Ph.D
Lecturer, East Asia School of Theology, Singapore

ENTRUSTING
the Key

From serial dating to
joyful waiting

ALI SMITH

IMPRINT
EDITION

Entrusting the Key: From serial dating to joyful waiting
Copyright © 2010 by Ali Smith

Published in Singapore by
IMprint Edition
Campus Crusade Asia Limited
My SingPost Box 880052
Singapore 919191
Fax: (65) 6262 3613
Email: info@crusademedia.com.sg
Website: www.ccalmm.com

ISBN-13: 978-981-08-5959-6

Some of the names of persons mentioned in this book are changed for anonymity.

Cover design: Ken Yuktasevi
Cover photography: Ruth Soh
Interior design: Chelsea Tay

This title may be purchased in bulk for business, educational, fund-raising or promotional use. For more information, please email info@crusademedia.com.sg.

A portion of the proceeds from the sale of this book will go towards providing college scholarships for street children in the Philippines.

*To my twin sister, Kelli,
who kept me company in the womb,
and who continues to keep me company through
the precious seasons of life.*

As Paul prayed so beautifully for the Ephesians,
I kneel before our Father and pray,

"...that out of his glorious riches he may strengthen you with power through his Spirit in your inner being, so that Christ may dwell in your hearts through faith. And I pray that you, being rooted and established in love, may have power, together with all the saints, to grasp how wide and long and high and deep is the love of Christ, and to know this love that surpasses knowledge—that you may be filled to the measure of all the fullness of God.

Now to him who is able to do immeasurably more than all we ask or imagine, according to his power that is at work within us, to him be glory in the church and in Christ Jesus throughout all generations, forever and ever!"

~ Ephesians 3:16-21

Amen.

Contents

Foreword by Susan D. Hill ix

Author's Note: An Invitation xiii

Introduction: A New Season xv

PART I: LEARNING TO WALK

1. The Canvas of My Past 3
2. Taking God Out of the Suitcase 9
3. Serving My Heart on a Silver Platter 13
4. Accepting Closed Doors 19
5. Giving My Own Green Light 25
6. The "List" 31
7. The Center of His Palm 37
8. "Just Friends" 43
9. Positioning to Receive 47
10. Thank God for Godly Counsel 51

PART II: LEARNING TO TRUST

11. Point of Surrender 61
12. Blessings of Obedience 63
13. Waiting in Action 67
14. A Game of Seek-and-Find 73
15. Holy Guacamole 77

16. Be Content, Not Confined 83

17. Skype Dates with God 87

18. Refusing the Pressure Cooker 93

19. Awed by His Awesomeness 97

PART III: LEARNING TO WAIT

20. A Good Laugh 105

21. Staying on the Potter's Wheel 109

22. Not Every Man You Meet is a Potential Mate 111

23. Serendipity 117

24. Lonely but Not Alone 121

25. Total Life-Sharing Intimacy 127

26. A Lesson on Yokes 131

27. Signs or Insanity? 139

28. The Ministry of Marriage 145

29. Soul Mates: A New Perspective 151

30. Finishing the Race 155

Conclusion: His Beautiful Bride 159

Reflection & Discussion Guide 177

Notes 191

Acknowledgments 193

About the Author 197

Foreword

by Susan D. Hill

*O*ver a decade ago, Ali Smith joined a small Bible study I hosted for high school girls. Our group met in a cozy guest house on the property of a wealthy family near a lovely farm pond. We made hot cocoa with marshmallows and talked about salvation, sexual purity, forgiveness and intimacy with God. Yet, it felt difficult to engage these girls for two hours each week, knowing that a culture of disrespect, casual sex, parties, and relative truth worked on them day and night, undermining everything I tried to impart.

The group dissolved as they headed off to college, and soon after I learned that almost every one of them had compromised sexually and drifted away from her faith in God. I felt completely disheartened and grieved for years, weeping in prayer for those girls. My best efforts seemed so ineffectual. The roar of the culture had drowned out the message and blessings of knowing God.

Ali Smith was an exception. As a teen, she experienced a new hunger for God. Tiny seeds from our group discussions took root and flourished during her college years. She is now a woman after God's own heart who longs to share her experience, strength and hope. I have seen the radiance on her face and know this book is just the beginning.

Ali understands the stigma singleness can carry in a world obsessed with love-at-first sight and happily-ever-after fairytales. And she knows in the deepest sense that we're all single. From our conception, God woos us to ignore worldly distractions, push past mere religious experiences and seek a love even beyond human relationships. He's intent on being the primary focus of our attention and love. And all for our benefit.

As a single woman in my college years, I chose Jeremiah 17:7-8 as a life verse: "Blessed is the (woman) who trusts in the Lord and whose trust is the Lord. For (she) will be like a tree planted by the water, that extends its roots by a stream and will not fear when the heat comes; but its leaves will be green, and it will not be anxious in a year of drought nor cease to yield fruit" (NASB).

These words struck a chord with me as I navigated the ups and downs of dating. Purity wasn't the only thing at stake. I gradually learned that God had to be my source of well-being and my sense of identity.

We cannot depend on physical appearance or prowess. We won't find security in accomplishments, education, financial standing or marital status. But if we grow deep roots in God and what He says about who we really are, all our endeavors and relationships will be different. We will have less to prove, less to hide, less to fear and less to lose. We will develop equilibrium and wholeness. We will be grounded despite a dysfunctional society that advertises its insecurities and constantly checks its sex appeal in the bathroom mirror.

God starts by inviting you on a morning stroll. After awhile He takes you over a few hills and up out of a valley or two. You may continue with Him, jogging a few miles or hiking up a narrow path to a ridge. You will have sore muscles, and wonder how you managed. Yet your confidence in the One leading you will grow, because you really get to know someone on a trail. The hikes will get steeper and more precarious; the cross-country jogs will become longer, requiring extra endurance. You may do a marathon or even a triathlon, knowing God is by your side.

And then the day comes when it becomes clear that all this training has prepared you for a new frontier called Marriage. In the beginning, it doesn't feel much harder than a day hike, but God knows better. He describes it as mountaineering, and says it's the kind of journey where you'll have to keep going, even when you come to the end of yourself. But don't flinch. God will make the trip with you, just as He has all along.

Most couples say "I do" and saunter down the aisle with no concept of what lies ahead. Many are unprepared to the point of feeling bamboozled later. God takes husband and wife down to the core of their worst selves in order to heal and rebuild two people into one. Marriage is His instrument of radical transformation. What you build with God in your single years is therefore all-important and will carry you throughout your life, especially if marriage is in your future.

T. S. Eliot said, "We shall not cease from exploration, and the end of all our exploring will be to arrive where we started and know the place for the first time." From a Christian perspective, though we begin in God and end in God—there is a vital journey in between.

In these pages, Ali Smith articulates her exploration of singleness with remarkable authenticity and her trademark passion. As she invites you in on her "Notes to Self," you can find the intimacy with God she's found along the way. It will change everything.

I know. It has for me.

Susan D. Hill, Author
Closer Than Your Skin: Unwrapping the Mystery of Intimacy with God,
WaterBrook Press/Random House, 2008

An Invitation

There, I did it. I entrusted the key to my heart into God's hands. As I sat there alone at the kitchen table in my Singapore apartment, I realized the significance of what I had just done. I was saying, "Here you go God, take control of my love life." Not only would this mean that I would trust Him to protect my heart and keep it safe, but that He would be granted full access to perform "heart surgery," preparing it to love and receive love from a spouse some day. A spouse that He would choose.

Don't worry. It took me a quarter of a century to get to the point of totally surrendering my heart to Him in the area of relationships. That's what this book is about. I share my journey of learning to hear, trust, obey and wait on God to direct me in the way to go regarding matters of my heart. In these pages you'll find a compilation of personal reflections, stories, insights, and prayers, many of which were taken from my private journals. I've also included Scriptures that have had a powerful impact on my faith journey along the way. While the experiences recounted are uniquely my own, I believe the deep longings of my heart are universal. I don't claim to be an expert on this subject, only a fellow traveler.

Perhaps the words on these pages will touch you, resonate with you or challenge you in some way. Good. Take them into your own prayer closet. Chew on them. Wrestle with them. Meditate on them. Ask God for further understanding or deeper insight within your own soul, on your own road.

My heartfelt prayer is that this book will leave you thirsting for the deeper things of God. That you will have a new and growing desire that burns from deep within—not to seek after the perfect mate, but to seek first a relationship with our Father, whose voice is as real and tangible as the person next to you. He is true to His word, which says, "Whether you turn to the right or to the left, your ears will hear a voice behind you saying, 'This is the way, walk in it'" (Isaiah 30:21).

And finally, I pray that this book may encourage you that it is possible to "entrust the key" to your heart to God, even in this increasingly modern world in which we live. There's no formula. No format. Just simply making the choice to trust in His ways and follow them with your whole heart. This will bring you into His resting place, full of peace, hope and joy. A place free from fear and worry over matters pertaining to your heart. A place where you can wait patiently and expectantly for our Heavenly Father's pick of a spouse in His appointed time—if that is His will. The question is, are you willing?

You don't have to know the answer yet. Just come, exactly as you are, whatever your relationship history or current relationship status may be. I invite you to my table to feast on a bit of my journey. The only requirement is that you come hungry and thirsty with an open mind, a willing spirit and an expectant heart. A heart ready to taste that the Lord is real and the Lord is good. Exceedingly and abundantly more than all we could ask for or imagine.

Introduction

A New Season

There is a time for everything,
and a season for every activity under heaven.
~ Ecclesiastes 3:1

*T*he Season of Singleness: I'm sure it's not the first time you've heard that phrase. It probably won't be the last time, either. That was the title of a church talk I once attended. I would always go to these things in hopes of gaining some fresh insight into the topic. After all, I was a 25-year-old single Christian woman with a desire to get married some day.

But as the speaker touched on the same "buzz words" I had heard a million times, "Guard your heart...be equally yoked...desires...don't settle...wait on God's timing...etc." it was as if my heart was lulled into some kind of stupor.

These were indeed Biblical principles, parameters and guidelines laid out by God relating to love, dating and relationships, meant to help guide us into godly relationships. Yet it seemed they had morphed into a long list of Christian clichés, falling on deaf ears—mine included. It wasn't that I didn't *want* to be led by God in the area of relationships— I did. I wanted to trust that He would bring the right person along at the right time. I wanted to have the patience to wait. I just didn't know how.

In essence, I had the head knowledge, but I yearned for more depth on the practical side: What did it really mean to be equally yoked? How was I supposed to guard my heart? What was I supposed to do while I waited? How was I supposed to know if I was settling for less than God's best?

It wasn't until I was alone in my room the very night of that talk when God began to reveal a deeper truth about this so-called "Season of Singleness" in which I was living. The words to my favorite worship song came on. I started singing along: *"Jesus, I wanna sit at your feet... take a drink from your cup. Lean back against you and breathe...feel your heartbeat. This love is so deep...it's more than I can stand. I melt in your peace...it's overwhelming."* [1]

I remember sitting there pondering this love that was "so deep and overwhelming." I imagined myself literally sitting at the feet of Jesus. Then I imagined taking a sip from His cup. I leaned against His chest and drew in a deep breath. I felt warm and safe in His arms. I suddenly felt so close to Him, it was as if I could literally feel and hear His heartbeat. I sat there, allowing myself to revel and rest under the blanket of His love. All my problems, my fears, my worries seemed to melt in His presence.

It may sound strange. Believe me, it was strange for me too. In all my years growing up in the church and with God, I had never been touched by Him quite in this way before. I had always prayed to God and knew He loved me from what the Bible said. But this was different. This was a God who embraced me, held me and interacted with me. His presence was real and tangible, and it brought with it a kind of transforming power that seemed to be seeping into every fiber of my being. I felt like a magnet being drawn to His side.

That's not all. In the midst of this encounter I heard the Lord's whisper, "Now this is what this season is all about, Ali; getting close to Me." Wow. Just hours before, I had been yawning in my chair, trying to keep interested in the all-too-familiar "Season of Singleness" spiel, wondering if I would ever be able to walk with God in the area of relationships. But suddenly here I was, face to face with God Himself, hearing the voice I had longed to hear, regarding not only matters of my heart but every area of my life. I was tasting what intimacy with God could be like and I wanted more.

From a Season of Singleness to a Season of Intimacy with Him. That's my story.

PART I

Learning to Walk

The Lord makes firm the steps of those
who delight in Him;
though they stumble, they will not fall,
for the Lord upholds them with His hand.

~ Psalm 37:23-24

1

The Canvas of My Past

No winter lasts forever; no spring skips its turn.

~ Hal Borland

*I*t all started in the 5th grade. It was a cold winter day in snowy Montana, when my twin sister Kelli and I sent each other on a mission: to ask our respective crushes to "go out" with us—the term we used in the 5th grade when we liked somebody.

Kelli went first. I remember feeling the pang of nerves and anxiety, as I waited for her to return from the field where the boys were playing football. My thoughts were racing as she asked my crush, Jesse Miller, to be my boyfriend. *What will he say? What if he says no?*

After waiting for what seemed like an eternity, I saw Kelli skipping back to where I was on the monkey bars. Luckily, she was wearing a smile—*a good sign*, I thought.

"Well?" I asked trying to keep my cool, as if I didn't really care either way.

Her hesitation made my hands sweat. "Well…" I was convinced my twin was purposely drawing out the suspense. "He said yes, Ali. Yes!" I let out a sigh of relief as we jumped around in celebration.

Then I was off to ask her crush, Ian O'Reilly, the very same question, to which he also answered, "Yes."

By the end of the day, we both had our very first "boyfriends." A new and unfamiliar wave of excitement came over me. My adventure of love had begun.

———•—

Our hearts always start with a blank canvas. Layers of color and texture are added as the years go by. Our thoughts, attitudes and ideas about relationships, dating and love take shape at a young age as we see, hear and observe the natural environment around us.

I share snippets of my upbringing and early relationships because they are some of the major scenes that unfolded in the original setting of my life. They were the layers of color—of observation and experience—that were added through the years. What my little eyes saw as a child and what I experienced as a young adult influenced my perspective regarding matters of the heart.

I was fortunate to grow up with parents who loved each other. They showed affection towards each other and said, "I love you" often in front of us kids. Though I didn't realize it as a child, their shared faith and value system was at the center of their relationship. They believed their marriage was more than a legal arrangement, but a spiritual union bound by God's love and grace—for life. It didn't come without its ups and downs, but they always instilled in us kids the value of commitment to one another. I remember my dad saying once, "Every day I wake up I am faced with a choice: will I love your mom today?"

Though my understanding as a child was limited, it was in these moments I remember feeling safe…knowing that my parents loved each other and were willing to do what it took to remain committed to each other.

I suppose observing the ways in which my parents related to each other during the eighteen years I lived at home influenced my own thoughts about marriage and relationships. As I became an adult, I never feared marriage or commitment to another person. In fact, I've never thought twice about whether or not I even wanted to marry. It just seemed the natural thing to do.

It wasn't until my second year of college that I actually pondered what it might look like. I was at home for summer break and my younger sister startled me with the question, "Do you think you'll marry Tom?"

Tom had been my boyfriend for two years. We had met during my second year at Princeton. We shared many things in common and had tons of fun together. He made me laugh more than any other person I knew. He loved to read and get into intellectual discussions about random things. He was the captain of his athletic team. Basically, he was an all-around great guy.

But the only answer I had for my sister was, "I don't know... maybe." It was the first time I had ever imagined a future with someone. Growing up in a culture where dating was the norm, I had liked a lot of different guys during my high school and early college days. Some of them were mere crushes, while others developed into relationships over a span of months. My approach then was sort of like test-tasting a big box of chocolates: you take a bite and put it back if you don't like it. I had some fun relationships on various levels of seriousness, but none of them were ever geared towards a life-long commitment.

I remember lying in bed that summer night after my sister had asked if I thought I would marry Tom. I realized I was no longer a teenager frolicking carelessly from one infatuation to the next. Nor did I want to be. I could definitely sense a shift in my heart, wanting to consider life for the long term.

The breeze was coming through the window, and I could hear crickets outside—a familiar sound that reminded me of my childhood running free through the Montana countryside. I felt wedged in a crevasse, between childhood and womanhood. I longed for the simplicity of childhood, but I couldn't deny the new pulls and pulsations of my heart, as it grew more attached to Tom. New questions burned from within, *Will Tom be the one I will marry?* A new shade of color was being painted onto the canvas of my young heart, and I wasn't sure what to make of it.

When I considered a life with Tom, there was one issue that kept gnawing away at my heart from the inside: faith. We shared common values, but our approaches to our faith in God and our expressions of it were drastically different. He had grown up in a Catholic family. The God he knew was distant. He only went to church on major holidays and didn't see a reason to go otherwise. He told me he didn't pray and for him faith was about trying to be a "good person." There wasn't anything wrong with his approach to his faith; it was just different from my own.

I had grown up in a Protestant, church-going family. My parents instilled in me the importance of going to church regularly and engaging in our faith community. We were active in Sunday school, youth group and summer Bible camps. We prayed at the dinner table and were taught to pray before bed. For us, being a Christian was more than a religious obligation; it was a relationship with God through the person of Jesus Christ.

Talking about God or anything spiritually related with Tom either led to awkwardness or petty arguments. In the end, we just "agreed to disagree" and resolved to seldom talk about God or share any thoughts on our faith. While this was fine in a college setting, I wondered how this might come into play in dealing with real life issues like how to handle finances, resolve conflict and raise children. What then? Sharing the same faith with a spouse might not be a value important to everyone, but I couldn't imagine it any other way. Perhaps it was because of my upbringing, but I could see the value in it. When it came to making big decisions or coping with difficult situations, my parent's shared faith and dependency on the same God was the glue that held them and our family together.

After two and a half years of dating, my relationship with Tom ended. Though I felt it was the right thing for both of us, it didn't come without consequences. My heart had grown so attached to him that it was painful to pull apart. It was enough of a stinging heartache to make me want to be more cautious the next time I was going to consider a relationship for the long-term. Whoever that person would be, I realized that sharing the same faith was definitely something important.

I didn't yet know how to respond to these newly-forming convictions, and God had not yet given me the words to articulate them. All I knew when I graduated college, was that He had some important lessons to teach me. I was to learn them in a foreign land far from anything I had ever known.

2

Taking God Out of the Suitcase

By God's grace, I stand on tiptoe, viewing all His wonders grand,
praising Him who freely gave me simple faith to understand.

~ Bosch

*I*f it were up to me I would have been working in New York City after I graduated from college, along with the majority of my friends. That was the safe option, even the preferred one. But instead, I listened to a soft little "nudge" deep down inside that led me to accept a fellowship through a program called Princeton-in-Asia. As the name implicates, it's an organization which sends fresh college graduates to Asia to live and work in various sectors. I was posted to Manila, Philippines to work for a news network there.

The next thing I knew, I was landing in the sprawling archipelago of more than 7,000 islands. I had no idea what awaited me. I knew no one. It was my first time living on my own, my first real job and my first time in Asia. As I rode in a taxi from the airport to my new apartment in Manila—jet lagged from the nearly 24-hour journey—I suddenly realized I was entering into something so far outside my "comfort zone" that part of me wanted to ask the taxi driver to turn around and head back to the airport so I could hop on the next flight back home.

Looking back at my high school and college years, my "comfort zone" had consisted of living in a community where people knew me and I knew them. Things like family background, interests and personality were known entities among close friends, so there was seldom a need to question or explore the deeper side of things. I enjoyed life in my so-called comfort zone until one day, the topic of God came up in casual conversation with a friend and she said, "Oh, I didn't know you were a Christian, Ali."

I remember mulling over this comment for days. In fact, I was deeply troubled by it. This had been a friend who had known me for a couple of years. How could she not know I was a Christian? This was a huge wake up call for me, which birthed a new question: If I say I am a Christian, what should my life look like? While I was a "churched" believer who did church well, I realized that outside that world, my life at that moment didn't look any different from anyone else. My beliefs weren't being reflected in my everyday life.

I had treated my faith, in a sense, as an item in a suitcase. If I was going to fellowship group or to hang out with another Christian friend, I would take God out and put on my "Christian identity" for that short time. And I truly enjoyed this identity, having fellowship with other Christians and talking about spiritual things. But when I was around my non-Christian friends, my faith went back in the suitcase shoved under the bed. It wasn't something I purposely or consciously did. It was simply the result of not knowing who the "real" me was.

I didn't know it at the time, but God was going to catapult me halfway across the world to show me. He was going to bring me to a place where I could finally take Him out of the suitcase and learn to wear Him 24/7. He was going to show me what a life in Him really looked like.

It was just a few days after I arrived in Manila when I felt God giving me an opportunity to respond to the prospect He had laid before me—to give my entire life over to Him. It was my *23rd Birthday* and I was all alone. It was the most alone I had ever been in my life. But oddly enough, I didn't feel alone. This was the first time I could really recall a tangible feeling of God's presence with me. I couldn't deny the tender and compassionate invitation coming from the Spirit of God Himself. That's when I found myself getting on my knees and praying this heartfelt prayer,

> *Dear Lord, I thank you for bringing me to Manila. I have no idea what's in store for my future, but I really feel You are with me and You are inviting me to know You more. I am sorry for carrying You around like an item in a suitcase all these years. Lord, this moment I want to wear You as a garment, never taking you off ever again. I invite You into my heart to change me and help me live for You. Jesus, I believe in my heart that You died on the cross to save me so I could have a vibrant, living relationship with our Father God. I really don't know what this means or what it looks like. All I know is that I want my identity to be rooted in You. Take the reins, Lord, and help me to trust You in all things. Amen.*

Something happened when I prayed that prayer in my room... something supernatural that I couldn't even put into words. All I knew was that it set in motion a process of internal transformation. The eyes of my heart were enlightened and I suddenly knew the hope to which He had called me through Christ (Ephesians 1:18). I believed with new conviction that faith in God went beyond practicing a religion, to knowing Him personally and letting this permeate into every area of my life and being.

This transformation, however, did not happen overnight. Taking God out of my "suitcase" to become fully clothed with His new identity meant I had to go through a process of shedding my old skin. God needed to remove old habits and attitudes that were keeping me from living a life that reflected His love in me.

I liken the experience to watching my precious nephew, Abe, learn to walk. He went from crawling to discovering a new and wonderful world he could see from a standing position. In the early stages, his mother (my twin sister) would stand behind him holding out her finger in front of him, so he could use it as a balance. She had to let him stumble a few times, but my nephew knew she was always there to catch him, to comfort him and strengthen his confidence so he could one day walk on his own.

Just like my nephew, I had been crawling through life and relationships for too long on my own, with a limited view of what life with God could look like. It was time to learn the "spiritual walk."

As you will see in the following chapters, I had to stumble a few times before standing on my own. But my loving Father was always there to pick me up.

3

Serving My Heart on a Silver Platter

Those who do not really believe God speaks specifically will simply ignore
or explain away all the times when God does communicate with them.
However, those who spend each day in the profound awareness that
God does speak are in a wonderful position to receive His words.

~ A. W. Tozer

My first few weeks in Manila went surprisingly smoother
than expected. I attribute it to the warmth and hospitality of the Filipino
people. They were so willing to open their homes to share their family,
food (yum!) and cultural heritage with complete strangers like me.

I was having dinner with the family of a colleague just weeks
after my arrival. They were curious as to how I was adjusting to the
Philippines. Then the two teenagers sitting across the table started
giggling and whispering, until one of them finally asked, "Any Filipino
suitors wanting to court you yet?"

The entire family, Lola (grandma) included, burst into a fit of
laughter. Meanwhile, I was trying to diffuse the question just thrown

my way, *Suitors? To court me?* They were speaking English, but it was as if they were speaking a different language altogether. Seeing that I was totally lost and in a bit of culture shock, this family graciously explained to me how this custom of "courtship" had been adopted in Filipino culture from the Spanish colonizers in the 16th century. A Filipino man, or suitor, was expected to work hard to win the love of the woman (and her family) before she would agree to have a relationship with him. This would inevitably lead to Filipino men singing romantic love songs, writing letters, giving gifts, or finding some way to "prove" their affection. The Filipino woman being pursued however would play "hard to get"—what was seen as an appropriate behavior to be able to measure the sincerity of her admirer. Some courtships could last years before the woman accepted the man's offer of love. This so-called practice of courtship still exists in Philippine society, though to varying degrees.

As I listened to my Filipino hosts, I felt for a moment like I had been transported back to the Middle Ages. Parts of it seemed a bit whimsical and slightly outdated but something about two people taking time to get to know each other through the various stages of courtship—involving family members and close friends in the process— seemed right. It sought to uphold and preserve a woman's value and worth in a way that seemed to be disappearing in the modern context of the dating world—at least the one in which I had grown up.

I had yet to be courted the Filipino way, but there were some men that came into the picture soon thereafter. It was only then that some of my faulty attitudes about relationships and the pace, at which they should happen, were brought to the surface.

One day, my friend came racing up to me after a church service, "Ali, I have someone I want you to meet." This Filipino friend had somehow morphed into my personal relationship agent. Since he was already engaged and about to be married, he took it upon himself to play "matchmaker" for me and others. As a 23-year-old single woman, I was never one to turn down an opportunity to meet someone new.

"Okay, sure." I said, "Who is it this time?"

"Well, let me give you some highlights. He's American, like you. Ivy Leaguer, like you. Basketball player, like you. Christian, like you. And the cherry on top—he's tall, like you," he said, winking. ·

This profile looked a little more promising compared to my less than favorable experience I had had with Filipino prospects up to that point. Let's just say when you're a gargantuan behemoth of a woman towering over half of the male population, romantic sparks don't exactly fly with ease.

That next week, my match-making friend arranged a bowling night out with a big group. The man of mystery I was supposed to meet, Alvin, was there. We had a ball of a time (no pun intended) and when the night ended, he offered to drive me home. It was supposedly on his way home, but I later found out it wasn't. Whether he was interested in me I had no clue, but he had clearly taken the chance for us to get to know each other a little bit.

However, my forthcoming American-self missed out on this key word, "little bit." On the drive home, I found myself spilling my whole heart to this guy I hardly knew. I went on and on about my family, my faith, my interests, hobbies, goals and dreams. I basically unleashed the whole "Life Story of Ali Smith" in less than a half an hour. I put my heart and soul on a silver platter and served it all in one course.

I remember getting out of the car that night and having this feeling of exhaustion. I felt like I had just completed a marathon—with my mouth. My brain and heart almost ached from sharing so much from those deep places of my heart. Something in my spirit was stirring. I couldn't shake this feeling that perhaps I had stepped outside of God's boundaries, though I was still learning what those boundaries were.

I began to seek the Lord for understanding on this. That very night, I wrote in my journal:

> *Why, God, am I so eager to pour out my whole heart and soul to a guy I barely know? Am I desperate? Am I impatient? Am I trying to discover if this guy could be 'the one' in one night? Am I trying to know things before you have revealed them? Please help me understand why I did this!*

God began to show me it was all of the above. He reminded me that my heart was special and should be treated with the utmost care and respect. That meant carefully considering to whom I serve it on a silver platter and how much at a time. A seven-course meal was not served all at one time. Rather it was served in increments, so that each unique course could be fully savored and enjoyed. In essence, this was the whole idea behind courtship too—enjoying the process of getting to know someone over a period of time.

Through the car ride experience, God not only exposed my longing for intimacy and relationship with another person, but also my tendency to try to make it happen too fast. God was telling me, "Whoa, easy my child, put on the brakes!" There was a lot He still needed to teach me about some of the learned behaviors and attitudes regarding love and relationships I had picked up over the years. My conditioned heart needed to be restored back to its intended health and wholeness before I was ready to share it with someone else. It started with getting to know Him.

During this season of singleness, I could see that I needed to redirect my desires. God wanted me to go from seeking fulfillment and worth in men, to seeking wholeness in His loving presence. He was calling me to His side, saying, "Come my daughter, let me show you what true intimacy is all about."

In the end, nothing developed past friendship with the guy who drove me home that night. But meeting him revealed some weak areas that God wanted to work on. It also brought a fresh and powerful new revelation of God's love for me.

It was time to let God court me—Filipino style.

4

Accepting Closed Doors

Most often the Word of the Lord comes to a soul
in the ordinary duties of life.
~ Anita Brechbill

*I*n the weeks following the motor-mouth episode, I continued to seek to know more about God through reading Scripture and spending time with friends who shared my hunger to grow spiritually. In the process, God was gently revealing things about myself and shedding light on certain habits and ideas about my life that were completely opposite of the way God intended me to live. The verse in the Bible that says, "Whoever is a believer in Christ is a new creation. The old way of living has disappeared. A new way of living has come into existence" (2 Corinthians 5:17, GWT) was becoming a reality in my life. This "new way of living" was becoming apparent through the people and circumstances He placed around me.

One day, I received a text from my friend Tina, "He's here! Bringing him to church. See you there...." She was referring to her nephew, who she had been telling me about for weeks. He was moving to Manila from California to start up a new business. From her description there was definitely some potential—Filipino-American, grew up in California, basketball player, worked for a real estate company, loved God.

I arrived at church and spotted them immediately across the sanctuary. The service seemed like it took an eternity to end. But when it did, Tina dragged him over as soon as she saw me.

"Ali, meet my nephew Adam. He just moved to Manila from California. Maybe you could take him around and introduce him to your friends." Her overly eager enthusiasm made things slightly awkward and embarrassing. I don't think she could have been any more obvious.

"Sure, I'd love to." I muttered nervously, trying to act casual and nonchalant. The truth was that my heart was beating so fast I could hardly focus on what we were saying. Not to mention my legs grew weak, softening like warm noodles in a bowl of spaghetti. I literally had to give myself a silent pep talk, "Pull it together Ali!"

Luckily, my less than stellar first impression didn't ruin everything. In the following weeks Adam and I hung out in groups going to dinners, movies and bowling. We were having a lot of fun with each other, but I was unclear in which direction it was heading, if any. I started to pray earnestly for God to show me His will for our friendship. I asked God point blank, "Lord do you want us to explore this beyond friendship?" Asking for guidance before I dove head over heels into something was new for me.

One night, a group of us were supposed to have dinner. At the last minute, everyone backed out—except Adam and me. The place we had planned for dinner had a nice, cozy and some might even venture to say (ahem) romantic atmosphere. We were seated upstairs where there were lounge-style seats and low tables, lit with candles. It was never supposed to be a date, but it sure seemed like it by the looks of the setting.

We ended up having a great evening full of conversation and laughter. At one point I remember thinking how I could totally picture us as a couple. I know the waiters serving us already thought so. I may have been reading too much into it (not that women ever have that problem), but it certainly seemed like something could have been developing between us.

At the end of the night, he drove me home. Though I would have never said it aloud, I was secretly waiting for him to launch into some romantic soliloquy, pouring out his feelings for me. But my hopes were shattered when we pulled up to my apartment. He gave me nothing to work with. As in *nada*. Zilch. Only a little tap-tap on the back followed by a, "Well, take care!" The buddy-buddy ring to it made me cringe. My heart felt like it had just dropped on one of those multiple-storey free-fall rides.

I sat in my apartment that night mulling over the dismal farewell. *Take care?* I even tried to rationalize it; *maybe he's just putting on a front. Yep, I bet he's just playing hard to get.* Just as my thoughts were about to spiral out of control, the Spirit of the Lord stopped me, reminding me He was there to listen. I wrote this prayer in my journal,

> *Lord, I thank you for the enjoyable evening that Adam and I had tonight. Lord, does he like me??? I pray Father that you help me to keep my emotions at bay so I can see clearly and tread carefully. I pray Lord that I may see this friendship as you see it. I feel so tempted to open my heart Lord. I feel like a child with a piece of candy being dangled in front of me but not being able to eat it. It's not a pleasant feeling Father. I don't like feeling my heart's desperate vulnerability. Keep it protected and*

safe in your hands. Lord I ask that you either open the door or shut it with Adam. I mean that. I love you. Amen.

A couple of days after I prayed this prayer, a group of us went out to dinner. It was a mix of girls and guys, some of whom I knew previously and others I was meeting for the first time. I tried my best to save a seat for Adam next to me, as he was coming late. By the time he showed up there were no seats open near me, so he took a seat at the opposite end of the table.

I was trying to stay attentive to the people who were sitting around me, but I couldn't help but notice the flirting going on at the other end of the table. Adam was clearly having a grand old time—with someone else.

He wasn't doing anything wrong. After all, we hadn't defined anything. But I couldn't fight a sinking feeling in my heart. I thought for sure there had been something developing between us, especially after our dinner alone together a few nights before.

I excused myself to go to the bathroom just to take a few deep breaths. I felt hurt and disappointed. But as I sat there alone in the bathroom stall, I suddenly recalled my prayer to God a few days prior, *Lord, if this is not your will shut the door. I mean it.*

Oh man. I wondered if it was possible to retract words already spoken to God. Couldn't I just erase them and pretend this whole thing never happened? Then God could simply reverse the situation and we could go on living happily ever after? Sounded like a good plan to me.

But God clearly did not agree. It was as if He was challenging me right then and there: "Do you really mean what you pray?" As much as I wanted to take it back and say, "No Lord, I didn't mean it… I take it back!" I knew deep in my heart that this was in fact God answering my prayer that not only came from *my* mouth, but *my* heart. I had meant what I prayed.

All I could do was yield to God closing the door on this one. There was a momentary boo-hoo, but mostly from my bruised ego. The neat thing was that God totally changed my heart after that. The attraction I had felt for Adam was suddenly removed. My mind, too, was free from all the thoughts and questions of what we "could have been." As I sought to honor God with my life by obeying His instructions, I felt He honored me in return with clarity, peace and freedom to move on. God was telling me to keep moving the Ali-train forward, "It's not time for a stop yet, my dear."

A closed door isn't always easy to accept, especially when it's on something that we want, or we *think* we want. But I was learning to trust that when God is in charge, sometimes one door has to close so another can open.

5

Giving My Own Green Light

For the Word of God is living and active...
it judges the thoughts and attitudes of the heart.

~ Hebrews 4:12

*I*was really enjoying my time in the Philippines. I had made a number of good friends who were also Christians. I felt like I was getting the hang of the way things were done in Filipino culture. God continued to place opportunities to learn to hear His voice of guidance and instruction.

This came in the form of yet another friend trying to "set me up." He thought his friend Joe, a Filipino, and I would make a great match. He was one of the leaders of the young adults' ministry at his church and a very active member in the community. He also trained regularly for triathlons and lived an active lifestyle. Not to mention he owned his own business and was very driven in his work.

We finally met one night at a friend's going away party. In the Filipino culture, this is called a "*Despedita*." We stood in one corner of the outdoor venue the entire night talking to each other, mostly about things that related to our spiritual life, like how we came to our faith, which churches we attended, where we were serving, etc. I remember being impressed by his level of interest in my life, which was different from many of the men I had met at other social gatherings. Rather than being concerned about looks or status or any of the more superficial aspects that often creep into the relational equation, he spent a significant amount of time asking about the street children's program in which I was involved. He wanted to know all about it. His genuine interest was a refreshing change.

The engaging conversation continued over a few dates. It wasn't until around the third or fourth one that he suddenly became quiet, "I have something to tell you."

"Okay…what?" My heart felt a sudden pang, like it had been stung by a jellyfish. My nerves were rattling, as he took a breath before speaking.

"I have a nine-year-old daughter." His voice was shaking as he looked me straight in the eye.

Gulp. The mutual friend who set us up had left out this minor detail. Not that it was a bad thing, but it definitely added a new variable to whatever we had going on…a big scary variable. I was a 23-year-old fresh college graduate and nowhere near ready to take on this kind of responsibility.

He went on to explain about the long-term relationship he had been in before he had come to his faith in God. His daughter stayed full time with the mother, but he spent time with her every other weekend. He said he understood if I wanted to stop seeing him.

Stop seeing him? Just the thought of it left a giant lump in my throat. In the few weeks of spending time with Joe, I had really grown to like him. I loved the way I felt when I was with him. It felt good to have someone again. I felt safe. Secure. *No way*, I thought, *this can't end.*

The emotional desires of my flesh overruled any clear-headed thinking. Without even consulting God, I gave my reply to Joe on the spot, "It's okay. We can make this work."

He looked relieved. But he also made sure I was certain about my decision to continue things with him. Without a second thought I replied, "Yep, I'm sure."

After this, our relationship took a sharp turn down Serious Lane. It was as if we pressed the "fast forward" button and accelerated everything. We had fun together and enjoyed many of the same activities. He was a committed Christian, and I loved that about him and our relationship.

But after a few months, questions began to fill my mind. For the first time, I actually pushed the "pause" button on our emotionally charged relationship screen and considered what a life with Joe in the Philippines might look like. What would it be like to inherit a nine-year-old daughter as my own? Could I do it? What would my parents think? Was this God's will for me? I told God that if it was indeed His will, then I was willing to say yes.

Then the Spirit spoke to my heart, "My child, you already said yes."

I retraced back to the night I had met Joe. I hadn't even asked God whether I should go on dates with him. Then, after Joe had told me about his daughter, I had let the loud "thump-thump-thump" of my own heart's throb drown out the voice of my Father.

God was right. I had said "yes" to this relationship on my own accord. I dove head in, fully engaging my heart, before He had given the green light. After this sobering revelation, I couldn't ignore the prompting to end things with Joe. He was a great guy, but God was telling me that I wasn't ready for this kind of commitment yet.

Once again, I had inflicted more damage to my heart. For weeks after the break-up, I cried myself to sleep at night, missing Joe. When you spend so much time with someone you get used to their smell, their voice, their laugh, their text messages and calls. My heart literally ached.

Along with that, there was also a grieving of the loss of the *idea* of Joe. I realized that liking someone at this age was not something to be taken lightly—unlike high school, when liking someone was an "in the moment" affair with essentially no thought or concern for the long-term future. Now, it involved the person *and* (for women probably more than men) the hope of what it could lead to. Breaking up with Joe was like a double whammy.

I was reminded of the verse that says, "The one who sows to please his sinful nature, from that nature will reap destruction; the one who sows to please the Spirit, from the Spirit will reap eternal life" (Galatians 6:8).

It really was true. My motives for being with Joe were not spiritual ones. Just because two people are committed Christians, as we were, did not mean we're exempt from seeking to please our sinful nature. I could see that with Joe, my motives were of my flesh, letting the emotional "feel good" overrule the spiritual "feel God." It was sowing in that nature that reaped the pain of a broken heart.

The consequences to my own actions were real and God allowed them. But more importantly, He revealed to me why the break-up had been so painful. Being with Joe exposed my being controlled by the needs of my flesh, seeking to find hope, security and safety in someone other than God. I had formed a dependence on him to be filled and fulfilled. But God didn't want me to depend on anyone else, but Him. He didn't want me to be secure in anyone else, but Him. The only true and lasting fulfillment would come from Him and Him alone. I had to learn it the hard way, but the message was getting across.

I didn't know how, but I knew He would help me get there. For God himself says, "I am the LORD your God who takes you by the right hand and says to you 'Do not fear; I will help you'" (Isaiah 41:13). It was through these very words that I heard God say to me, "Ali beloved, come, I will help you trust Me and follow My ways, so that I can answer every desire of your precious heart."

God was there all along, wanting to give me specific directions, telling me which way to go and with whom, when to pull over for a stop and when to keep moving. But instead of letting Him lead me, I had been too busy dragging Him along.

It was time to wait for the next green light—from my Father.

6

The "List"

So many of us limit our praying because we are not
reckless in our confidence in God.
~ Oswald Chambers

$\mathcal{B}$reaking up with Joe was difficult, but the spiritual rewards that followed from obeying the Lord in that decision were an unexpected blessing. I was learning to depend on God in all things, rather than human relationships. As I continued to direct my longings and emotions of my heart towards God, I was reaping the rewards of joy, peace and security in Him. This is when the Lord began to speak to me more directly about the desires of my heart.

It all started one ordinary day when I was checking my email before I went to work. I was having a blast working as a news reporter and anchor for the English-speaking news channel in Manila. This particular day I was rushing to make it to an interview, so I had time only for a quick check. But the following message in my inbox threw me for an unexpected loop:

Hi Ali, I was awakened in the night and felt compelled
in my spirit to write you. I felt (from my conversation with

God) that you should pray for your future husband. If you don't already, pray for him. Not just to be delivered into your hands (haha...) but for his life, his heart, his walk, etc. And for all the things you want him to be, as well. The Spirit also said to me that He's going to give you the desires of your heart. John 15:7 says, "If you remain in me and my words remain in you, ask whatever you wish and it will be done for you." So don't be shy Ali. Ask! Love, Anne

It's not every day you get a message like that. Anne was a good friend of mine, whom I had gotten to know during my stay in Manila. She and her husband were posted there through his company for a couple of years, like me. The words from her email that seemed to jump from the computer screen into the inner chamber of my soul were, *pray for your future husband...and all the things you want him to be.*

This was a new concept for me. I had always prayed before going to bed, or when I needed God's help on something, but seldom for the longings inside me. And if I did, it usually would be something like, "Lord, I hope it's in your will for me to get married some day. If it isn't, then I know Your grace is sufficient. But Lord, if possible, please don't make me a lonely old maid." In other words, besides the occasional pleas to God—that I would not remain single my whole life—I didn't really see the point of praying any further. I sort of felt it would just "happen" when it happened.

Then, the very next week, another friend in my Bible study group continued to challenge my prayer paradigm. She was driving me home and out of the blue asked me, "Ali, have you told God what kind of husband you want?"

I was shocked. It was as if she had read the email my other friend had sent me just days before. I wondered if it was possible that she had secretly hacked into my Gmail account. Then I realized how ridiculous that was and attempted to answer her question, "Um...is it up to me to decide what kind of husband I want?"

She went on to tell me her story, how she had sat down before God and made a list of characteristics and attributes that she desired in a life partner. "Though some are called to a life of singlehood," she explained, "the rest of us are called to marriage. Asking God for a spouse is asking Him for something He created and called very good." And she added, "God really did give me everything I prayerfully asked for, right down to the thick black hair!"

At that time, I wasn't sure how I felt about the whole "list" thing. It seemed to me like parents picking the traits of their child before the baby was born. Besides, I believed God knew what I needed, much more than I even did. Why the need to voice my wants, wishes and requests like a child would to Santa Claus before Christmas?

As I persisted in my skepticism, God continued to persist in getting His message across. The following week, another friend (in a completely unrelated situation), asked me the very same question about whether or not I had made my "list."

I didn't even hesitate this time, "No, I haven't," I said, confident in my stance.

"Why not?" she prodded. This was a woman who also had a success story of asking God for certain specific things that she desired in a mate and God answering every one of them.

She explained further. "Ali, it's not so much about the list itself. Rather, it's the practice of committing certain areas of our lives to prayer—praying for them consciously, consistently and persistently—so that we can give God the glory when He answers. I believe God puts desires in our hearts so we will come to Him and ask for their fulfillment."

Clearly, God wasn't going to let me shove this issue under the skeptical rug any longer. It was time to start praying specifically and asking for things that were already in my heart. But I was still wrestling with how to do this. How was I supposed to know if my "desires" came from God or my own flesh?

A particular friend, whose list was so stringent, came to mind. It included things like ethnicity, income bracket, job, academic achievement, among other things. I had watched her turn down man after man who didn't have every little thing on her list. It seemed to me that her being so specific could have been preventing her from getting to know potentially great and godly men God was putting right in front of her nose. It's not to say God wasn't capable of the impossible. But at what point are we just being picky?

One night shortly thereafter, as I was praying one of my generic prayers, I heard the Spirit say to me, "Why do you come to my table as a beggar for breadcrumbs, beloved, when I have an entire feast for you?" Wow. That one knocked me out for a while. While I had basically scoffed at those around me who had been making what seemed like unrealistic requests, God was telling me I was guilty of the opposite extreme...asking for too little. I realized right then and there my sights and expectations needed major readjusting when it came to asking from God.

My not asking wasn't because I trusted that He already knew what I needed (as I told my friends), but because on some level I think I feared that somehow my requests would be unacceptable to God. I worried that they might be too grandiose or vain. But as John 15:7 states, if I "remained" in God—pursuing, seeking and deepening my relationship with the person of Jesus through His Word—then I didn't have to worry. I could be confident that the things I was asking for were in line with His will.

For the first time, I began to think seriously about the desires of my heart, beyond the general ones: to love and be loved, to marry and to have children. God was challenging me through the testimonies and encouragement of godly women around me to press deeper into my desires. What kind of person did I envision spending my life with? What would his passions be? What was the calling over his life? What would he look like, even?

The Lord was teaching me to confidently talk to Him about these things and not treat them like some beggarly issue. God had put individual desires in me and wanted to see me walk them out—for His glory. An article I stumbled across put it like this, "When you're living like you're planning to marry, being intentional about discipleship, and looking for ways to support those around you in their roles, then you can pray boldly. For those who are called to marriage, such prayers are nothing more than asking Him to give us what He wants you to have."[2]

I felt I had no other choice but to respond to this revelation. One night, soon after I received all these related messages, I sat in my room and prayerfully wrote out a list of everything my heart desired in a husband. Admittedly, it was kind of scary at first. But as I asked the Lord to help reveal to me, through His Holy Spirit, things that He wanted me to desire in a life partner, it became easier. And He also nudged me not to hold back.

I wrote out the following "list" in my journal,

1. *Love for God drives his life*
2. *Lives by the Word of God in every aspect of his life*
3. *Has a teachable spirit, desiring to grow deeper in the things of God and become more like Christ throughout life*
4. *Has a passion for souls and ministering to the lost and broken-hearted*

5. *Values going to church and engaging in the faith community*
6. *Has leadership qualities in the workplace and home*
7. *Wants to "be fruitful and multiply" (raise up godly children!)*
8. *Loves to travel, meet new people and experience different cultures*
9. *Gifted communicator*
10. *Sense of humor—doesn't take himself too seriously*
11. *Values health, fitness and active lifestyle*
12. *Tall, strong, manly, athletic (Lord, you told me not to hold back!)*

I was learning not to be embarrassed to admit my desire for marriage. The few women God put in my path encouraged me not only to acknowledge my hopes, but also to pursue them through prayer. I felt a new freedom to really pray.

> *Dear Lord, thank you that You correct me so that I may enjoy a more satisfying relationship with You, my Abba Father. I am sorry, Lord, for coming to You as a beggar for breadcrumbs. Please give me the confidence and the boldness to ask for what my heart desires. Thank you that You created this desire for marriage for my good and Your glory. I don't know Your time-line, but I ask that You prepare me to be a godly wife as I trust in Your ways. Thank you that wherever my husband may be this moment, You are preparing his heart to do Your will too. And that one day we may enjoy a feast at Your table—together. Amen.*

God helped me to break out of my "beggarly mindset," no longer weighed down by doubts that what I wanted was good. As I grew closer to Him, my heart's desires were naturally being meshed with His. All I had to do was remain in Him.

7

The Center of His Palm

Be strong and courageous. Do not be terrified; do not be discouraged,
for the LORD your God will be with you wherever you go.

~ Joshua 1:9

*M*y time in Manila was coming to an end. Though it had
been a wonderful two years, I was ready to move on. I prayed to God,
"Lord, I'll go wherever you want me to go—whether it's back home to
the U.S. or somewhere else in Asia. Wherever you open doors, I will
walk through."

Several job interviews later, I was presented with the opportunity
to move from Manila to Singapore to work for an English-speaking
news network there—for another two years. I had meant what I said
to God, that I was willing to go wherever He wanted me to go. But
as the contract lay in front of me demanding a signature, fears and
reservations suddenly flared up.

Did I really want to sign up for two more years away from my family? Would this have a negative impact on my friendships back home? And another pressing question coming from both me and my loved ones back home: How would I ever find a husband in Asia?

Around this time, a dear American friend who was also living in Singapore sent me an article about a National Football League (NFL) player, who spoke out about his faith and serving in Christian ministry together with his wife. She had typed in the subject line of the email: *We're DOOMED.*

What she meant was that there were no such men in Asia. This friend and I had always joked that we hoped to marry "big, strong, manly" men (with faith in God of course), just like the football player in the article. It was probably because we were both former athletes ourselves—she had played volleyball at UCLA and I had played varsity basketball at Princeton. Our whole lives we had grown up being bigger, taller and stronger physically compared to most women, which was a good thing—when it came to sports.

But living in the real world, in Asia, we felt like giants next to the tiny frames of our Asian friends. Though we had accepted the fact that we would never be considered "petite" (sigh), we figured we could at least create an illusion of feeling smaller by marrying larger men. However, these larger men were few and far between in the part of the world in which we were residing. If I chose to stay in Asia, maybe my friend had been right: *I was doomed.*

All joking aside, what was really at the root of all this was the fear of not being in the "right place at the right time." All my friends back home in the U.S. seemed to be finding their "Mr. Rights." I wondered if staying in Asia automatically meant putting these desires on hold, or even worse, missing out on them altogether.

During this time of experiencing fear and doubt, I became even more transparent with God. The following is a prayer I poured out to God in my journal:

> *Lord, if I stay in Asia, will I be single forever? I feel like you are telling me to stay here but what if I miss out on meeting people in the U.S.? All my friends are dating and meeting people and I'll be stuck here alone. Should I move to a place where the chances of meeting and marrying someone I am attracted to are higher?*

I still had a week before I had to give the news network in Singapore my answer. I wanted to be absolutely sure before I committed another two years of my life to living in a country half way across the world from my homeland.

That's when God swooped in and sent one of His "angels" to encourage me. It came unexpectedly, as Words from the Lord usually did. A friend and I were having coffee one ordinary day and I don't remember what had launched us into the topic, but she started sharing a story of a woman she knew, who had been scared to accept her call to go live and work in India as a missionary. The woman was fighting "the call" because she feared that if she went to India, her desires to get married and have a family would never be realized. She was in her mid-thirties, so she knew if she were going to have her own children it would have to be soon. Then the woman had the following dream and this is how she described it:

> *I saw myself sitting in the center of the palm of God's right hand. In His other hand, I saw a man, also sitting in the center. Though I couldn't make out the face of the man, I knew in the dream it was the man God had for me to marry. Then, I saw God's hands moving together and when they touched, God took my hand and put it in the man's hand. He then released*

us together, hand in hand, into our united calling planned out for us....

The woman awoke knowing that the Lord was speaking to her through this dream. She interpreted it as the Spirit encouraging her to stay in the center of His will, no matter where it was. God knew every desire of her heart and nothing—not even geography—could keep Him from answering them. That was enough to nudge her into obedience, and off to India she went.

To make a long story short, she eventually met her husband, who was also a missionary who also obeyed the call to India around the same time she did. They married and began raising a family together while honoring their call to serve in India.

This beautiful testimony reminded me of God's faithfulness. I realized I had been limiting God's greatness and power by believing He could answer the desires of my heart only if I was in the right country at the right time. But the God of this woman's vision was the very same God I served. This meant that He did not move on account of geography, but of proximity to Him.

A wave of comfort came over me as I considered moving to Singapore. Though there were many variables and unknowns, I knew deep down that this leap of faith would keep me right in the center of God's palm.

The voices of doubt inside of me were silenced as I pulled out the papers for my two-year contract. I signed them with a new sense of confidence that I was hearing and following the voice of my Father. I felt God working through my hands as I put the ink to paper. I whispered, "I trust You are in this decision, my Lord."

This was a prayer I wrote in my journal after I signed my contract:

Dear God of yesterday, today and tomorrow, thank you that Your love is unfailing and Your ways are unchanging. Father, I confess my temptation to want to take control of my life, letting fear rule, choking out Your love and its power. Forgive me God, and help me to trust You more and more. Thank You for placing the opportunity to move to Singapore in my path, challenging me to take active steps of faith, even when it seems terrifying. I trust that You are on the other side of this decision. Lead me on Your path of righteousness and never let me veer from the center of Your big, warm, safe palm. Father, I lift up the man whom You have just for me, who is in Your other palm and I thank You for giving us the patience and the peace to wait on You to bring us together, releasing us hand in hand into a life with You. May Your will, not mine, be done in Jesus' name. I love you. Amen.

The direction in which I was traveling was not totally clear. Nor did I know exactly how my future was going to pan out. But I was discovering that obedience didn't require a full understanding of things. Obedience was trusting Him, even when I couldn't see with my human eyes what was up ahead.

God's words were going beyond my head knowledge and sinking into the depths of my soul. They were becoming real and living experiences in my life. I could perceive God's rich and tender love for me as He gently instructed me in the way to go. I knew I would be safe, as long as I kept walking with Him…side-by-side.

8

"Just Friends"

Listen to my instruction and be wise; do not ignore it.

~ Proverbs 8:33

When I moved to Singapore, the only other person I knew, besides an American expatriate family, was Charles. I had met him through my former boss in Manila. I would be forever indebted to him because he had helped me land my new job by connecting me with one of his friends.

Charles went out of his way to make sure my transition to this new place went smoothly. He was a native to Singapore, which meant he was privy to all the special "nooks and crannies" of the foreign city I had just moved to. He showed me some of the local food joints in Singapore, known as "hawker centers." Overwhelmed at the plethora of choices—*satay*, chili crab, noodles of every kind, chicken rice—he would order a bunch of things to share. Not exactly good for my waistline, but it was fun to try the best of the local delicacies.

Singapore is one of those cities where people dine at all hours of the night. Eating is a social thing to do among friends. In Southeast Asia, Singapore is known as the ultimate "foodie" paradise. And I must say it lives up to the reputation! Over several late-night outings with Charles to these food centers, I discovered he was very engaging and interested in a range of topics that also interested me. Did I mention he was also an ambitious entrepreneur with a vision to change the world, very handsome and single? Even so, I really hadn't thought of him in any other way besides being a friend, whose company I genuinely enjoyed and was grateful for.

Before long, we were spending every waking moment together. When I wasn't with him people started asking where he was, as if they expected us to be together. Our friends started to assume that we were an "item." By the looks of it, they were right to assume. But we weren't even thinking of it—we were "just friends."

One night we were out late having coffee and dessert, to get our last fill of conversation before I left for a two-week trip to the U.S. The moon was out, leaving a beautiful reflection over the water in front of us. Christmas lights were all around. Everything seemed so easy when we were together…so comfortable. I loved it. He dropped me off at home and we parted with a goodnight kiss on the cheek, "See you in two weeks!" I walked away with a smile on my face, thankful I had such a good friend to come back to.

When I was away those two weeks, I missed Charles. I found myself constantly calculating the time difference, thinking of what he might be doing back in Singapore. On Christmas day, he was the first person that entered my mind to call. My family even questioned whether there was something "more than friends" going on between us, because he had come up in so many of my stories as I shared about Singapore.

I hadn't realized what a big part of my life he had become until that visit home.

I had gotten so used to his presence that not having him there felt weird. It was like enjoying a cup of coffee every morning and then suddenly cutting yourself off, going cold turkey. You don't realize your body is addicted to the caffeine until you cut it out. In the same way, I didn't realize I had become "addicted" to my daily cup of Charles.

I had no idea whether or not he had even noticed or cared about my absence while I was gone. But for me, missing him like I did suddenly created a cloud of confusion over our "friendship" status. My thoughts were bouncing back and forth like a game of ping-pong. *Am I just missing a friend? Or is there something more than friendship developing? No, we're just friends…but maybe there could be something… no, that might be weird.*

I brought these questions to God in my journal.

> *Lord, what is your purpose regarding our friendship? Is this a relationship that You intend to bring beyond friendship? Father, I come to You with a heart of sincerity and purity, and I ask that You help us to protect our hearts. Bring us clarity in this situation and convict us if we are stepping into territory outside Your will. Lord, I pray Paul's prayer in Colossians, that You may give us wise minds and spirits attuned to Your will, so we can acquire a wise understanding of the ways in which You work. Show us how You are working in this relationship, my Lord. Amen.*

When I returned to Singapore I was eager to see Charles. I was still unable to discern my feelings, but I hoped he at least shared some of my sentiments.

The next day we met. I shared with him openly what was on my heart. I told him how I had missed him when I was home in the U.S.

and how I didn't know what any of it meant. I wasn't looking for an immediate answer, but deep down I was secretly hoping he would say, "What a relief, I feel the same way!"

My eyes were locked on his as I waited for his confirming reply. And then he said, "Ali, I really see you…" *Yes*, I thought. *This is all going just as I hoped.* And then his final words hit me like a ton of bricks, "…just as a friend."

I must have looked like a statue because I didn't move a muscle. I couldn't believe what I was hearing. Did he really just articulate the word "just?" In that moment of humiliation, I wanted to freeze time, go backwards and start the conversation over again.

I thought back to all the times he had grabbed my hand to cross the street, or called late at night just to "talk." My friends had even hammered into my head, "He is sooo into you Ali, it's obvious." I wondered what had gotten lost in translation. Had I read too much into his actions? Or had I been misled? What seemed like obvious signs of interest to my friends and me had clearly been mere simple gestures of friendship to him.

I didn't quite know what to make of the situation. I think I was still in a state of shock that there had been no reciprocation on his end. All I could do was sit there in front of him, mustering up all the human effort I could to try to play it cool, while deep down I felt like a complete fool. I felt naked, as the vulnerability of my heart was fully exposed.

I had the sense that my friendship with Charles was crossing into some sort of Danger Zone, with a sign that read, "No More Trespassing." It was time to learn a little something about guarding my heart.

9

Positioning to Receive

Teach us to number our days aright,
that we may gain a heart of wisdom.

~ Psalm 90:12

$\mathcal{C}$harles and I continued to keep a close relationship, spending a lot of time together. I thought that since we had "cleared the air" in terms of our feelings for each other, we could go back to being just friends. As if my heart had a switch that I could flip "on" or "off."

It wasn't until I was praying before bed one night that the Lord dealt with me on this friendship matter. I suddenly heard the small still voice of the Holy Spirit whispering, "Ali, how are you spending your time and with whom?" Just like that—simple and to the point.

After a few moments of thought, I realized just about every single activity outside of work was spent with Charles—movies, dinners, and even church. Our "friendship" involved extensive time talking and hanging out one-on-one. We had a deep knowledge of each other's personality, hopes and interests. We would also share aspects of each other's daily lives and routines. No matter how clearly we had defined our relationship as "just friends," our actions were communicating a different message to our peers and our community.

At that time I was already seeking direction from God about my desire to marry. I had been praying and asking for a godly man, a life partner, a person with whom I could build a life together. It was as if God was calling me over for a sideline chat, "Pssst Ali, I want to answer your prayer, but you've got to get in position to receive it."

In position to receive it? I wondered what the Lord meant. What I discovered was that God was asking me to evaluate my own behavior and how I was conducting myself. I realized that I appeared to be tied down already—to Charles. From this position, it would be difficult to receive what He ultimately wanted to give me—a real and committed relationship geared toward marriage. I was like a child accepting a sugar-free lollipop: it looked like the real thing, but in the end it didn't even come close to the richness and quality of flavor. In other words, by choosing to remain in this intimate friendship with Charles, I was basically settling for a counterfeit imitation of love. God wanted to give me the "real deal," but I was settling for the cheaper version.

The wise words of Solomon further spoke to my situation, "Above all else, guard your heart, for it is the wellspring of life" (Proverbs 4:23). To continue sharing every detail of my life with Charles, knowing full well that it was not going to go past friendship would not be guarding my heart. Solomon put it this way: "Do not awaken love before it so desires" (Song of Songs 8:4). God was telling me not to awaken too soon the desire for intimacy He had put inside of me, for He intended them to be enjoyed within marriage.

This message rang loud and clear in those deep places of my soul. I didn't necessarily like it, but I knew it was a gift of truth wrapped with His divine wisdom. I had to take responsibility and make some changes in the way I was spending my time and with whom.

It was only through God's strength that I was able to make some purposeful shifts in my priorities and behavior. Charles and I had to allow some healthy distance to come back into our friendship. God helped me set practical boundaries, like no more talking late at night on the phone. I even asked a girlfriend to hold me accountable—whenever I got the urge to call him, I would call her instead. Our one-on-one time was also drastically cut down. If I was serious about what I prayed for, then some serious measures had to be taken, so that I could be in a position to receive from God.

God promises to "reward those who earnestly seek Him" (Hebrews 11:6). As I sought His help in this situation, He rewarded me with clarity and maturity to move forward from the friendship. He also gave me the strength and wisdom to stick to the boundaries I had set, which were necessary in order to keep my heart where it belonged—inside the protective gates of my Father's guardhouse, until He said otherwise.

This is a prayer I wrote in my journal after this huge learning experience.

> *Father, thank You for showing me that I have a part to play in being faithful to my own prayers and requests to You. Lord, help me orient my life during this season, in a way that is pleasing to You. Show me Lord, when I should engage my heart and when I should hold back. Keep me from awakening my desires for romantic love before it's time. May Your love be the only "filler" as I wait patiently, joyfully and securely in You. I lift up the person You do have for me and I ask that His heart and ears may also be open to Your love, teaching, correction and leading. I pray Lord that You are preparing him and positioning him to receive Your best for him too—me. Amen!*

I was learning that trusting God was more than following a book of rules and regulations, just for the sake of being a "good Christian." I was indeed following His Book, but it was from His very mouth that His words of loving instruction were now turning His vision into mine. My heart was being touched as He alerted me to new truths and gave me deeper insight into His character along my life's journey. This helped me to be more willing to trust Him with the entirety of my life.

Though it was not always easy, I understood that this was part of the process of transformation. He needed to perform radical surgery on my heart and my life, not to destroy me or my chances of happiness, but so that I could become who He intended me to be—whole in Him.

"Keep at it, Lord," was all I could say as my heart remained open to Him on the operating table. I wanted nothing more than a heart that was healthy and whole, reflecting His glory. From the inside out.

10

Thank God for Godly Counsel

Plans fail for lack of counsel, but with many advisers they succeed.
~ Proverbs 15:22

I often wanted spiritual maturity as quick as a cup of instant noodles. But unfortunately, there was no such thing as instant spirituality. God was in this process for the long haul and He was asking me to be, too.

Jesus often used the fermentation process and the aging of wine to explain this concept of maturation to His hearers. He would refer to a "wineskin," which was a leather bottle made out of a whole goat skin. Tied at the neck, it was used to hold grape juice until it was ready to drink.[3] As the fresh grape juice underwent the process of fermentation, the wine would expand, stretching the new wineskin. If the juice was poured out too early, the wine would be ruined. If it was left in the wineskin too long, the skin would burst, wasting perfectly good wine. It was only when the wine had fully matured and the wineskin was stretched just enough, then it would ready for us to drink and enjoy.

God was telling me that I was the wineskin, expanding and stretching as fresh grape juice—His Words—underwent fermentation inside of me. He seemed to be saying, "I am teaching you, maturing you, and making you whole." And in His perfect time, not a second too early nor a second too late, a matured wine would pour forth from my wineskin to be enjoyed with the person He chose for me.

In other words, there were no shortcuts for becoming whole, or mature in Him. I would have to keep living my life, trusting that God would continue to present opportunities to grow in my character and to grow closer to Him, through my ordinary circumstances.

There was one evening when a good friend from my fellowship group, Cory, invited me to dinner. We hadn't caught up for a while, so we made plans to meet and eat before the weekly meeting.

He went to the counter and ordered our sandwiches. When I reached for my wallet to pay for my meal (as any friend would), he stopped me, saying, "This one's on me."

Suddenly, my thoughts were racing, *Is this a date? Had I missed all the signals leading up to this point? Maybe he's just being extra generous. Or could it be…he's making a move?*

What I thought was just a friendship suddenly did a 180 degree turn. It was as if Cory transformed into one big ball of "potential" right before my eyes. I was surprised how with one small gesture, my own heart could flip flop like a pancake in a pan.

We walked to our table, sandwiches in hand. Now that I was on to his intentions, I suddenly became awkward. It was one of those times when in trying not to be awkward I actually became more awkward. I found myself blabbering about anything and everything under the sun, as I did when I was nervous. In the middle of my rambling about something that happened that day, he finally cut in, "Ali, I don't think it's any secret. I have feelings for you and I am interested in getting to know you more."

I took a huge bite of sandwich in an attempt to buy some time. *How do I answer?* I wanted to take another enormous bite, but realized that probably wouldn't be the best way to handle the situation. So I chewed extra slowly.

I was definitely caught off guard. But his forthrightness was impressive. He was so honest and composed—a refreshing change from the game-playing tactics of my past relationships. Or the lack-in-taking-initiative syndrome that seemed to be plaguing the modern church. And he was kind enough to say he didn't expect an answer right away.

Honestly, I didn't have an answer right away. In fact, I think I was speechless for a few moments after practically choking on my food. I thanked him and told him I needed to think and "pray about it." I was aware that this was a common tactic used by Christians in order to completely avoid a situation, but I meant it. I respected Cory and really wanted to hear from God on how I should respond. I felt like Saul when he was traveling on the road to Damascus and said, "What shall I do, Lord?" (Acts 22:10)

Cory had become a good friend and brother in the faith up to that point. I actually didn't know him *that* well, other than through group fellowship gatherings. I sought the Lord that very night when I got home, in my journal.

> *Father, I ask that You guide me during this delicate season. I know Lord that if I were to go on dates, my heart could get involved—even with someone You don't intend for me to be with. Lord, I don't want to over-romanticize, but I really do believe that You have someone who is Your BEST for me, according to what you have planned for me to do while on*

this earth. This is a major decision in life that will ultimately steer me in a certain direction. O Lord, I trust You to show me which man you would like it to be. Lord, if it is Cory, then open the eyes of my heart. If not, then preserve our hearts and our friendship. I love You so much Lord, I am Yours this day and forever. Amen.

The next day, I felt a prompting to contact my pastor's wife, Nancy, to seek her counsel on the situation. We often spoke on Sundays briefly after service, but I had never shared anything regarding such matters. I called her on the phone, admittedly a bit nervous. "Hi Nancy, its Ali. Do you have a minute to chat?"

"Well hi, Ali. Sure! What's up?" She had two little boys at home, whose needs I'm sure were calling for her attention. It meant a lot to me that she put everything aside to give me her full attention.

"Well, umm errr, there's this person. This guy. Well, he has expressed interest, but I am not so sure how to respond." I spit out some half-coherent words hoping they were enough for her to get the gist.

"Okay…" She was so calm. "How well do you know him?"

"Well, we attend the same fellowship group and we have a lot of mutual friends."

She cut straight to the nitty-gritty, "How do you feel about him?"

"Well, I really respect him on many levels. He's a great person and has a solid walk with the Lord. But I guess I am uncertain whether this respect is just a friend thing or if it could develop into more."

She went on to share about a similar experience she had encountered back in her single days (over 15 years ago), "Ali, whenever there was a guy expressing interest in me, I was grateful I learned the value of one thing."

"What's that?" My note pad and paper were out, so I could write down any words of wisdom that might help me wade through the murky waters of this situation with Cory.

"Time," she said. "Taking my time to make a decision about someone gave the Lord the opportunity to reveal His will in the matter. There was this one time a guy was pursuing me and I really couldn't discern my feelings for him right away. So I told him I needed time to pray about it. Within a week, he was already pursuing another friend of mine! That revealed to me where his heart was at. He wasn't serious about me after all, which I was thankful to learn through the simple passing of time, rather than finding out later when my heart was already involved."

It all made sense in my head. But the so-called "waiting game" was always easier said than done. "Did you find it hard to be patient?" I asked.

"You know what, there were times when it was difficult. But I really came to a point where I trusted God with my whole heart and I knew He wanted the very best for me. And let me tell you, it was worth the wait!"

"You mean because you met Pastor John?" This was the first time I was hearing how they got together more than 15 years ago. A bit strange, but intriguing nonetheless. It's always great to see the human side of pastors and leaders!

"Yes, I mean Pastor John. We were serving at the same church, but I wasn't even looking at him in that way—seriously. I'll spare you the details but eventually, the Lord changed our hearts towards one another and brought us together in His perfect timing. It really is a testament to the amazing way the Lord's will brings two souls together. When we have the willingness to wait for Him to show us, He'll show us. Period."

She went on to say she hadn't known the moment she met Pastor John that she would marry him, but through the passage of time and walking daily in obedience, God put a peace in her heart. And that became her guide in making decisions.

This was really resonating. "So I'm thinking of telling Cory that I really enjoy his friendship, but am not certain enough about my feelings at this point to engage further—what do you think?" I needed some sort of confirmation.

"I think that sounds like a wise decision, Ali. That way, you can still get to know him from a safe and healthy distance. As time passes, you can continue to ask God to confirm in your heart what His will for your relationship is. If it is just to be friends, well, at least your friendship will remain unharmed and you can trust that the Lord is preparing your heart to be with someone else, a little further down the road."

She went on, "Ali, when I was your age and wanting to get married, I trusted God with the key to my heart. He was the one who gave it to Pastor John when the time was right. And it was the best thing I ever did because he truly turned out to be God's best for me, even beyond what I could have ever hoped for or imagined. Truly! Just trust that God knows best.... He really knows best."

As I hung up the phone with Nancy, I picked it up again to dial Cory's number. He deserved an answer. I told him what was really in my heart—that I respected him greatly as a friend and brother in Christ, but that I wasn't certain enough about my feelings to explore anything further at that point in time.

Now, you may be thinking, "Gosh, so serious!" Maybe. But I realized that if I was truly seeking to be led by God in this area, as I was, and I trusted that God wanted to answer the desires of my heart, than that meant each person who God brought onto my path was to be treated with careful consideration.

Cory thanked me for my honesty and for respecting him enough not to have misled him. I'm not making the point that God is against dating altogether. In fact, the more I got to know God, the more I realized He wasn't real "religious" when it came to these things. It wasn't about obeying some rigid code of law just for the sake of it. Nor was He about following a formulaic one-size-fits-all path to marriage: "If you do A, B and C and you will be granted a husband." God was about relationship. It was from this place of knowing Him and loving Him that I could hear His voice, gently and wisely directing me in the way to go when it came to matters regarding my heart.

I had never really understood the value of godly counsel until this happened. I always hesitated to share too much with my church leaders and pastors, for fear of burdening them with things probably much less urgent than other matters crying for their attention. Though godly counsel doesn't have to come from an official church leader, I chose Nancy as someone who knew my values, my personality, and my heart. She was also someone who had lived the season I was in and had successfully made it through—God's way.

I realized in all of this that it could be hard to hear God's voice while drowning in a sea of emotions. Even the excitement of "possibility" with a person like Cory could have really thrown me for a loop. It's not to say God doesn't want us to enjoy experiencing the emotions that come along with being pursued by someone new. But emotions should never replace His directional wisdom and guidance in a situation.

Nancy, in this situation, was my "life boat," rescuing me from being tossed and turned by emotional waters, so I could see with clear vision. Her counsel helped me to navigate wisely, keeping my ship heading in the right direction.

PART II

Learning to Trust

*"The LORD is my strength and my shield;
my heart trusts in him, and I am helped.
My heart leaps for joy and I will give thanks to him in song."*

~ Psalm 28:7

11

Point of Surrender

Commit your way to the LORD, Trust also in Him, and He will do it.
~ Psalm 37:5 (NASB)

*N*ancy's last words to me over the phone the week before, played in my head like a broken record, Ali, *I trusted God with the key to my heart.* I wondered what it might mean to give God the key to my heart.

I began to explore the meaning behind the key image itself. The first thing that came to mind was security—a key was a way of locking up and protecting something of value. For example, I locked my apartment door when I leave each day as a way of preventing someone from harming or stealing the things inside. The second thing that came to mind was access. The key to my apartment allowed me to be able to gain access to the inside. The third thing that came to mind was that each key is special. Each apartment in my building for instance has a different key and only the owners of each apartment got the key to *their* apartment and no one else's. I would only share the key to my apartment with those who had my utmost trust.

That's when I was whacked with a moment of divine insight. God wanted me to trust Him enough to give Him the key to the "home" of my heart—so that He not only could protect it from harm, but also could gain full access to it, preparing it to love and receive love from a spouse one day. I had already opened my heart to Him, but I had yet to fully *surrender* it—especially when it came to relationships.

That's when it happened. I went into my shoebox-sized bedroom in my Singapore apartment, shut the door and got on my knees to pray,

> *Lord, I am sorry I have only been giving you partial access to the home of my heart. This moment, I am entrusting the master key to my heart into Your hands because I trust You. Please protect it, and prepare it until You decide who You want to open it. This is scary for me Lord, so please take away my fears and my doubts. I believe You know the desires from the deepest places of my heart and want to answer them. Show me how to live a surrendered life to You, O God. Have Your way in me, for I am Yours. Totally, completely and willingly Yours. Amen.*

It was in that moment that I put all my weapons down. I dropped all my guards. I let go of all my defensive tactics and completely surrendered. I don't mean to sound overly dramatic—like it was some scene out of a *Brave Heart* movie—but this was a turning point in my journey. Entrusting the key into His care was essentially saying, "Lord, take control of my love life."

And in the following chapters you'll see, He honored that request.

12

The Blessings of Obedience

It matters not the path on earth my feet are made to trod;
it only matters how I live: obedient to God.

~ Clark

Coming to this point of surrender—of entrusting the key to my heart to God—didn't mean I would remain locked up in an ironclad chamber until He hand-delivered Prince Charming to sweep me off my feet (though I would have gladly welcomed the fairy tale). It meant that I would be ready to seek His direction and guidance in my daily circumstances, so that He could further mold me into a woman who reflected His likeness.

Life as a news anchor and producer of both regional and international news programs was never dull. Every hour around the clock, there was a live show. It was a fast-paced and stimulating environment.

My shift during this period of time was from three o'clock in the afternoon to midnight, so I learned to squeeze in time with my friends whenever I had a spare hour—usually over lunch or a late "supper" (as they say in Singapore) after work.

One night, about a month after I had entrusted the key to my heart to God, I met a girlfriend after work over a late night meal. As we were busy chatting, filling each in on the details of our lives, I noticed a Caucasian man approaching our table.

"I overheard you saying you were from Montana?"

"Um, yes. That's correct," I smiled politely. My friend and I had been talking about where we had grown up.

"That's funny, I'm from Alberta." He was trying to make a connection between the two places—which aren't even in the same country.

"Oh, that's nice," was all I could think to say, since I knew next to nothing about Canada. Somehow the conversation continued, though. This guy was based in Hong Kong, working for a bank. He was passing through Singapore on business. Before he walked away, he asked if I would be interested in meeting for coffee or dinner the following day.

Based merely on externalities, Mr. Alberta had a lot going for him. He was tall (a unique find in Asia), well dressed, outgoing, apparently successful in his career. And like me, he had chosen to leave his home country to live and work in a foreign land.

Before deciding whether to accept his invitation for a date, I knew I had to take this home to my "prayer closet" for a consultation with my new heart manager, God. I prayed and asked if He was leading me into the situation or not. Did He want me to accept or decline the invitation? That night, I wrote this in my journal.

> *Lord, with my human eyes I see an attractive, successful, confident man. He is asking me out Lord and part of me wants to accept—just to see. But Lord, does He know You? Do You want me to go on a date with him? Give me Your eyes to see*

this situation and discern Your will. Speak to me and I will be quick to listen to You, whatever You tell me to do. I trust you! Amen.

The next day, he proposed to meet up but the time conflicted with plans I already had to meet up with another friend. I wondered whether I should cancel so I could go on the date.

I became still and silent before God. As I prayerfully pondered the situation, I felt the Lord saying to me through His Spirit, "Ali, if you honestly believe in your heart that THIS is my best for you...then go."

Wow. I knew this was from God because He is always a gentleman. He never forces me into obedience. He'll drop a question like this into my Spirit, giving me the freedom to choose. I ran through the scenario in my head, *Would cancelling another commitment to meet with a stranger who essentially used smooth tactics to hit on me late at night be God's best?*

My "old self" might have considered it. But somehow, I felt that God was telling me to keep moving. It's kind of like traveling on a train through Europe with so many sights to see—all are interesting, but this doesn't mean all of them merit a stopover. God was calling me to be a wise traveler on His love train, choosing carefully which "sights" (men) were worth stopping for a more in-depth visit. He was there to help me discern. All I had to do was ask.

I had my answer. I sent a text message reply thanking Mr. Alberta for the kind invite, but that I would not be able to meet him.

Hearing and obeying what I perceived to be the Lord telling me what to do, released a tremendous wave of peace into my heart. Though I didn't know one hundred percent that it was the right decision, I discovered that when certain actions were followed by the fruit of His

Spirit, like peace, joy, and self-control (Galatians 5:22), then I couldn't go wrong.

One of my housemates thought I was crazy for saying no to this seeming hunk of a man. "Aren't you being a little extreme, Ali?. I mean, what's the harm in going on one date?" She had a point. Maybe one date would have been harmless after all. Maybe it would have even been fun. But it was no longer about the date. It was about tuning in to the voice of my Father and wanting to follow His instructions because I loved Him.

I was reminded of Isaiah 55:9, where God says, "As the heavens are higher than the earth, so are my ways higher than your ways and my thoughts higher than your thoughts." Surrendering my heart meant that I also had to surrender my need to fully understand His ways. My job wasn't to try and figure God out. It was to follow Him. I am one of His sheep and He is my Shepherd, leading me in the way to go.

Saying "no" in this situation was saying "yes" to God, affirming my trust in His leading. His ways were indeed higher than my own, but they were also proving to work.

13

Waiting in Action

Waiting patiently in expectation is the foundation of the spiritual life.
~ Simon Weil

I walked into church one Sunday feeling tired and grumpy.
The seat I normally sat in—third row, left side—was filled. *Oh great,*
I grumbled to myself. I had to sit on the right side a few rows back, next
to a woman I didn't know who was busy wiping her child's runny nose.
It was a similar scenario happening in the row in front of me, behind
me and all around me. Rows and rows were filled with families with
children and couples holding hands, waiting for the service to start.
Meanwhile, I sat there alone, also waiting, but for God to bring me
into that "next phase." I wondered if the time would *ever* come.

Suddenly the woman next to me turned back around, "Hi,
there," she said, "My name is Patience."

Is she joking? I thought. The previous week I had been receiving
a whole slew of messages from God about "waiting" on Him. It started
with the words from a song I came across during one of my morning

devotions, "Take my spirit, Lord please fill it, with the patience *to wait on You.*" Then a few moments later, I opened my Bible straight to Psalm 24, "Make me know Your ways O Lord, Teach me your paths...*for You I wait* all day long." And to top it all off, when I had finished drying my hair and turned the hair dryer off, the song blaring from my laptop was Shane and Shane's *"I will wait on You, I will wait on You...."*

Coincidence? Perhaps, but I was learning that this was one of the ways the Lord made His voice known to me...through repetition. I don't think I could have created this clever sequence of related messages even if I had wanted to—especially not on a subject like waiting.

For lack of a better way to put it, I hated waiting. Whether it was waiting in a line at the grocery store, waiting for the outcome of a job interview, waiting for my next family reunion, or in this season, waiting on God to reveal when and who I would marry, it all seemed like nothing more than a helplessly passive and torturous state of having to wait on things outside my control to materialize, according to some mysterious divinely appointed time frame. I liked to get things done and in the most efficient way possible. I was one of those people who made "To Do" lists filled with petty little tasks to check off one by one, so I could enjoy the satisfaction of feeling "productive." I often wanted to apply the same approach to the desires of my heart:

"To Do" List for Ali's Heart:

    1. Meet my husband - check!

    2. Get married - check!

    3. Have children - check!

While efficiency seemed like the best plan of attack to me, God didn't exactly agree. He often required periods of waiting, which could easily transform into a very discouraging process at times. Especially in those moments like that day at church, when I felt the longings to share my life with someone well up inside me like a giant tsunami wave. These were times when all I wanted to do was march straight up to Heaven and shout, "Hurry up!"

Yet, throughout the history of the Bible, God's people had to pass through difficult periods of waiting on God for answers to different things. Even Jesus reflects a life of waiting. While He knew His ultimate destiny was to die on the cross, so all of humanity could be saved and have a relationship with God, He also understood specific events had to unfold, according to the perfect will and timing of His Father in Heaven. Entrusting the key to my heart to God meant simultaneously thrusting me into a life-long pursuit of waiting.

This prompted me to look up verses in the Bible where God speaks to those who are waiting. I wrote the following list of encouraging verses in my journal, so I could refer to them during difficult times:

"And not only so, but let us have joy in our troubles:
in the knowledge that trouble gives us the power of waiting;
And waiting gives experience; and experience, hope:
And hope does not put to shame; because our hearts are full of
the love of God through the Holy Spirit which is given to us."
~ Romans 5:3-5 *(Bible in Basic English)*

"Be waiting for the Lord, and keep his way;
and you will be lifted up, and have the land for your heritage:
when the evil-doers are cut off, you will see it."
~ Psalm 37:34 *(Bible in Basic English)*

"Do not say, I will give punishment for evil:
go on waiting for the Lord, and he will be your Savior."
~ Proverbs 20:22 *(Bible in Basic English)*

"Whoever keeps a fig-tree will have its fruit;
and the servant waiting on his master will be honored."
~ Proverbs 27:18 *(Bible in Basic English)*

*"And those who have knowledge of Your Name will put
their faith in You; because you, Lord, have ever given Your help
to those who were waiting for you."*
~ *Psalm 9:10* (Bible in basic English)

*"I am waiting for the Lord, my soul is waiting for Him,
and my hope is in His Word."*
~ *Psalm 130:5* (Bible in Basic English)

*"When I was waiting quietly for the Lord,
His heart was turned to me, and He gave ear to my cry."*
~ *Psalm 40:1* (Bible in Basic English)

*"Now may the God who gives comfort and strength in waiting make you
of the same mind with one another in harmony with Christ Jesus..."*
~ *Romans 15:5* (Bible in Basic English)

"Love is patient..."
~ *1 Corinthians 13:4*

*"And so, as the result of patient waiting,
our forefather obtained what God had promised."*
~ *Hebrews 6:15* (Weymouth New Testament)

Waiting was a part of the journey, I got that. But what was I supposed to do while I waited?

A quote by Henri Nouwen came to me in my inbox one day soon after God had started speaking to me about waiting, which said the secret of waiting was not passive at all, but active. Waiting for Nouwen was "...to be present fully to the moment, with the conviction that something is happening where you are and that you want to be present to it."[4]

I considered again the life of Jesus and could see how He was a prime example of being "present to each moment." He fully engaged in His surroundings—the people and opportunities put before Him. He had the conviction that "something was happening" where he was, as He made each moment count. This active style of waiting, we can now see, was not in vain!

This encouraged me that there were specific purposes God wanted to carry out even in my long hours, days or even years of waiting. While this season, I was waiting for a spouse, the next season it would be something entirely different. But choosing to trust that He was working through it all gave me new hope, and hope according to God's Word, "does not disappoint" (Romans 5:5).

It was as if God replaced my old dreaded paradigm of waiting with one from Heaven. Waiting wasn't something that God wanted to torture me with, but it was a great act of His love, so that I could be ready and prepared to receive His blessings and promises. The Apostle Paul couldn't have said it better, "The one who calls you is faithful and He will do it" (1 Thessalonians 5:24).

I began to ask God for wisdom in how to spend my time. He showed me how I could actively pour myself into my community, one day at a time, one moment at a time—like Jesus did. I volunteered to serve in the usher ministry at my church and as a prayer leader at my young adults' fellowship group. I also took time to pursue passions God had put in my heart, like running, writing and starting up a project geared towards helping impoverished youth in the Philippines. Living fully…present to each moment and trusting that God was working through it all…brought immense peace, joy and a sense of purpose that made the waiting period much easier to endure.

On the flip side, God also helped me to remove certain attitudes and behaviors that threatened to steal away the joy and peace He desired me to have while waiting on Him. Focusing on "lack," or what I didn't have, rather than what I did have was one example. I realized I could choose how to see my situation—dwelling on the fact that I was alone or grateful that I was surrounded by an abundance of friends that God put into my path to journey alongside me.

He also convicted me one time when I was complaining to some girlfriends how there seemed to be "no good Christian guys out there," and then proceeded to back it up with less than promising statistics about the unequal ratio of men to women in the church. But the Lord's voice came loud and clear to me after that, "Do you really trust Me?" Ouch. I realized the powerful impact my words could have in creating or destroying hope and joy in my community. If my words weren't going to build up or edify my sisters, God told me to leave them out, regardless what the "statistics" were. Trusting Him meant living by faith and not by sight.

I knew if I continued to wait like Jesus—living actively and purposefully in my present circumstances, then—I could trust that He was orchestrating all around me, even when I couldn't see it.[5] He had a plan that I may not have scripted, a plan that I may not understand, but it was His plan and His plan was good. The road could seem long and bumpy at times, but God wouldn't forget about me, leaving my heart's desires to shrivel up like a prune. I didn't yet have all the pieces to the puzzle, like the how-what-where-who, but I did have renewed hope—real, genuine hope—and excitement, not only for what the future held, but that I had confidence in the One who held it. He was in charge of "all things" and could be trusted to know what He was doing.

14

A Game of Seek-and-Find

Seeking God—intimacy with God—must be your priority.
~ Kay Arthur

*O*ne of my favorite games as a child was hide-and-seek. My twin sister Kelli was known for hiding in the most obscure places. We would search and search and search, literally tearing up our entire house, trying to find her. Eventually we got so tired that we would give up.

I think the Christian life can often feel like one big game of hide-and-seek. We search and search and search, struggling and straining to find God's purpose for our lives until the point of giving up. "If only I could find the Lord's will for my life!!"

I came to the realization though, that maybe it wasn't that God was such a good hider. Maybe we were simply looking in all the wrong places.

One weekend, I attended a seminar that started to point me to the right places. Though the topic of the seminar was prayer,[6] the speaker suddenly launched into sharing about her journey of seeking God and learning to trust Him, which was the key to enjoyment along her road of waiting for a spouse. "I gave it all to God when it came to my future mate," she said. "I knew He wouldn't leave me out to dry. I became so certain that God knew my future more than I knew my past. He knew exactly how my personality, skills and abilities would blend with a mate. I committed my ways to Him and let Him take care of the rest."

I suddenly wondered if she was wearing some sort of invisible "God goggles" that allowed her to see into the deepest crevices of my soul. I couldn't figure out why she had chosen to zoom in on this topic, even though there were all sorts of people in the room of various ages and stages. I felt as if she was speaking straight to the longings that had been lingering in my own heart. I was all ears as she continued to share about the wonderful game of seek-and-find she had learned to play with God. This woman had become a Christian in her twenties, but it wasn't until her late thirties that the Lord led her into marriage. Her season of waiting was certainly prolonged by most people's standards. I even caught myself uttering a quiet prayer to the Lord as she spoke, "Lord, please don't let that be me!" I suppose we're wired to think if we're not married by a certain age, we're doomed.

But this woman saw a great opportunity in her years of being single. She had more time and freedom to pursue God with her whole heart. "I learned to seek first His kingdom and His righteousness," she said, quoting Matthew 6:33, "and I knew that as long as I did this, all things—including every desire of my heart—would be given as well." Seeking first the Kingdom, for her, meant going deeper in her prayer life with God and spending more time in His presence. She cultivated a lifestyle of seeking after anything and everything that was of Him.

My mind chewed on her words like a piece of bubblegum. I was in awe of how she spoke with passion and certainty about the God she served. Out of her seeking came a vibrant and living relationship with her Father. Intimate and deep. Enjoyable. It was as if she was speaking about a best friend standing right next to her.

In the end, God did fulfill her heart's desire to be married and to be a mother. Just short of her 40th birthday, she met her husband at a conference. He was widowed with children of his own. Months later, they were married and she became the mother to four healthy boys to love and to raise as her own. "So trust our Father," she encouraged us, "He knows the right and perfect timing…and what it will look like."

It was after this seminar that I realized what an opportunity this unique season of being single presented—to seek first His kingdom and His righteousness in all things. When I wasn't busy at my day job, anchoring the news, I attended classes and seminars that would deepen my knowledge and understanding of God. I also devoted more time to seeking Him in my prayer—through the assistance of the Holy Spirit—which added a new richness and depth to my relationship with God. Out of this lifestyle of seeking grew precious fruits, like crisp revelations from His Word, an illuminated vision for my future and specific directions for my life.

There were certainly times when desires God had not yet fulfilled would bubble up to the surface of my soul like the white foam of a root-beer float. My heart longed to share my life with someone in marriage. I wasn't in denial of that fact. But just as the foamy substance eventually died down so you could get back to the best part of the ice cream-filled float, God would also always bring me back to the best part of knowing Him—a place filled with green pastures and quiet waters.[7]

A beautiful resting place of peace and surrender that said, "Lord, let Your will be done."

Ironically, I realized that the best thing in life wasn't even about having my heart's desires fulfilled. The best and most fulfilling thing was knowing I was on whatever path God had chosen for my life. As the Psalmist wrote, "You make known to me the path of life, You will fill me with joy in Your presence, with eternal pleasures at Your right hand."[8]

All I had to do was seek in the right places—and He could be found. Guaranteed.

15

Holy Guacamole

Jesus rarely comes where we expect Him; He appears where we least expect Him,
and always in the most illogical of ways. The only way a worker can keep
true to God, is being ready for these surprise visits.
~ Oswald Chambers

Mexican food was without a doubt my favorite food on the
planet. Tacos, enchiladas, beans, rice, guacamole—you name it, I loved
it. One evening my friends and I were having dinner at our favorite
Mexican restaurant in Singapore. It was the best I had discovered
during the entire three years I had been in Asia.

Just as I was about to dip my first chip into a huge bowl of
mouth-watering guacamole, the spirit within pulled me to a halting
stop. Half-way to the bowl, chip in the air, saliva oozing from the
corners of my mouth, it was as if everything around me went into
slow motion as God drew my attention to the green-avocado-salsa-
lemon-infused mucky mess that I loved so much. He was trying to
tell me something—apparently related to guacamole. But it wasn't
immediately clear what.

This rather odd encounter came just weeks following the seminar on prayer. I had been imagining myself in the speaker's shoes, regarding the way her marriage testimony played out. What gripped me was her openness in considering a man who was already a father of four children. Would I be ready to handle the responsibility of inheriting children to care for as my own? I can imagine this woman had similar fears and reservations herself. But she allowed God to help her move past them to see a man's heart. She saw a man who loved the children God had given him—a beautiful portrayal of our Father in Heaven. She also trusted that if God was calling her to inherit four children, He would enable her to do it.

I think God was drawing me to a level of trust in Him that saw beyond externals. And that's when the whole guacamole thing clicked—sometimes people's lives could look on the surface like pea-green guacamole, nothing short of a big pile of pooh, but the unique mix of flavors and spices gave it a uniquely exquisite taste unlike any other dip. Just as I had been willing to give guacamole a try, despite the looks of it, God was in some (odd) way telling me He wanted me to have a similar openness towards my future life partner. The analogy may have been a little far-fetched, but I could see the point God was trying to make.

This brought me to my knees as I realized I may have been guilty of devising a narrow-minded view of what a "godly" man's life would look like. I was reminded, too, of times when I had been quick to write off a person because he didn't "fit the mold" of the person I had imagined—outgoing, fun-loving, adventurous, athletic and a leader. Someone who wanted to make a difference in the world, speaking and influencing both young and old around the globe. Someone who wanted to conquer any mountain and be loud and bold in doing it.

These were traits and characteristics that I thought would gel well with mine—and perhaps they would. But God was challenging me to look at things a little differently.

I didn't know how to reconcile two very different paradigms circulating in my heart and mind. On one hand, I had been encouraged by other Christian women to "pray for everything you have ever dreamed of in a husband and don't settle for anything less." On the other hand, I had been told "not to overlook the ordinary-looking guy right in front of you." There had to be a synthesis between praying boldly the desires of my heart and still having a certain level of flexibility to yield to God's way of seeing things.

One night, I asked God to help me pray over the life of my future husband—from His perspective. I wanted His help in sorting out the difference between "settling for" and being "too picky." In the middle of my prayers that night, the Lord brought a question to my spirit, "Ali, are you the woman of God he is praying for?"

I thought for a moment about what God might be getting at. I believe it was sort of a "you are what you attract" type of thing. He was telling me that if I was desiring, expecting and praying for a man of God, then it was only fair that my life reflected the kind of woman he would be drawn to. God was shifting my focus away from what kind of man I wanted to marry and more towards the woman of God he wanted me to be.

When I came across words from a worship song called "Sanctuary," it was as if God was saying, "START HERE"—with a big fat arrow pointing at these lyrics:

> *Lord, prepare me to be a sanctuary,*
> *Pure and holy, tried and true.*
> *With thanksgiving,*
> *I'll be a living sanctuary for you.*[9]

A living sanctuary was God's standard—pure, holy, tried and true. I wondered what that might mean in a modern context. I imagined becoming a nun and living in a monastery. That idea lasted about two seconds. But I seriously wondered what living a "holy life" might look like from God's perspective.

I tried imagining my friends using such adjectives to describe me, "Ali, you're so holy. So pure and true." It was almost laughable in today's world, and yet God had called His children into a life of holiness. We're instructed to be holy, "as He who called you is holy" (1 Peter 1:14-16).

The very word "holy" conjured up some vague idea of spiritual perfection in my mind. However, a friend once said that holiness was not about reaching some sort of spiritual or moral perfection, but about "His holiness being perfected in us."

I liked that way of thinking of it, but allowing His holiness to manifest in my life would mean making choices that were aligned with His Word. As I devoted more time to prayer and studying His Word, I increasingly desired to do things that pleased God and to stay away from things that didn't. God's life and character were seeping into every fiber of my being, turning me into one big pile of holy guacamole—not perfect on the outside, but made of the finest ingredients on the inside—straight from Heaven's recipe book.

God was showing me that it was this holy guacamole kind of woman that a true man of God would be drawn to, whose inner beauty would outshine the outer appearance. I love the way Peter put it in his first letter to the early Christians, "*What matters is not your outer appearance...but your inner disposition. Cultivate inner beauty, the gentle, gracious kind that God delights in....*" (1 Peter 3:4, *author's paraphrase*).

Just as I hoped a man would be attracted to this inner beauty in me, the Lord was telling me to look for this inner quality of soul in a future husband. I was humbled by this reminder. I needed the Lord's help to be open to what a man of God might look like through His eyes, not through my worldly lens.

I wrote out this prayer in my journal:

> *Lord, I am sorry if I have diluted Your standard of holiness. Bring me back to Your standard, which is of a different kind and on a higher plane than the world. It's the kind of holiness with which Jesus lived, seeing inside of people's hearts rather than their external circumstances. Thank you Lord, that as You prepare me to be a sanctuary—pure and holy, tried and true—I will become the kind of woman you have called me to be. And that will be a godly woman, to whom a godly man will be drawn. Amen!*

I wanted to be like the woman who married the widowed man, who was not looking for a man of perfection by the world's terms, but a man perfected internally by His love. Her willingness to consider someone who didn't exactly fit the mold of the "type" of guy she thought she would marry turned into the greatest blessing. He was a great father, a family man and a true friend—traits that not only satisfied her needs but were pleasing to God.

I was determined to be more open to the men God brought into my life, asking God to give me spiritual eyesight to see beyond the external circumstances and into the heart. It didn't mean I had to stop asking God for certain characteristics I desired in a mate. But I realized these things should never be the end-all and be-all when discerning if someone would be a suitable life partner. It was about desiring a man who knew and loved God the way I did and being flexible enough to let the Lord show me what that might look like.

Even if it was a big bowl of holy guacamole, I was ready to dig in to taste and see the Lord's goodness working through another life.

16

Be Content, Not Confined

Cultivating contentment in the Christian life begins with
understanding that things never define your value.
~ Charles Stanley, *Into His Presence*, p. 120

*A*s months passed, more and more of my friends seemed
to be entering into the next phase: marriage. Almost every week,
a wedding invitation would arrive through the Singapore Post, "Save
the Date!" or "You're cordially invited to partake in the union of..." The
outside of my fridge became wallpapered with newlywed couples and
couples-to-be.

There is nothing more exciting than watching friends and
siblings take that "next step" with that significant other person. I truly
was happy for them. Still, there was a part of me fighting an internal
battle against one behemoth of a question, *When will that be me?*

At times it felt like everyone else seemed to be "graduating"
to that next level, wearing their caps and gowns as they screamed in

triumphant jubilation, "We did it, we did it!" Marriage marked the point of finally "starting their lives." Meanwhile, it seemed I had been left behind in the dust—alone.

We're programmed to think that real life begins when we have acquired certain things. In the United States, the succession usually looks something like: husband, dog, mortgage, kids, and the list goes on. In Singapore, I learned that the succession entailed the five "C's": career, condo, car, credit card, country club. It was easy to feel that my life—without a life partner or some of these other "things"—was somehow incomplete. As if everything had come to a grinding halt, and there was a large sign hanging over my head in boldface letters, "LIFE ON PAUSE UNTIL MARRIED." Was it true? Did I really have to wait until my knight in shining armor came along until I could live out what God has called me to do?

It wasn't until I went back to visit the Philippines that God exposed this line of thinking for what it was: a big fat lie. During the two years I had lived in Manila, I had volunteered for a feeding program called Street Dwellers Outreach Ministries Inc. Every Saturday morning, we would open the rusty gates of a small church in one of the poor urban areas, welcoming families from nearby shanty villages. It was a time of fellowship, food and fun—a break from the daily grind of street living. One small group of about 12 girls came back week after week without fail. The bonds between us grew strong during those two years.

I was hoping to see them during my visit. I got in touch with Alfredo, the former director of the feeding program, and asked him to arrange a reunion with some of the children. I was eager and anxious as I arrived at the planned meeting place. Before I knew it, I was being tackled to the ground, surrounded by giggling girls. I looked around and to my amazement, nearly every single little girl I had hoped to see was there! It was truly a heavenly reunion and one mightily answered prayer.

That night, I sat alone in my bedroom and wept. Tears of joy poured from my eyes as I remembered the beaming faces of the little girls. But the tears were also pouring out in response to the heavy burden of sorrow I felt for their futures, which looked so dire. I wanted to have hope but as snapshots of their dark slums burned into my mind; hope for these girls seemed impossible.

Bob Pierce, founder of World Vision, once said, "Let my heart be broken for the things that break the heart of God." My heart felt broken for these girls. Yet in the brokenness, I also felt God's overwhelming love for each little girl. Though I couldn't see the light in such dark places, God whispered something in my spirit that night as He dried my tears, "Ali, you are the hope I have sent."

It was in this moment that I felt God's gentle reminder that He had important things for me to do for Him—married or not. I could still fulfill His call over my life of being His hands and feet, delivering His help and hope to the lost and broken of this world—married or not. My life had indeed started and was unfolding fully and completely before my eyes—married or not.

My desires for relationship and marriage were still present, along with questions of when it would happen. But I wasn't consumed or confined by them. My life was being lived out to the fullest, despite the fact that those things had yet to come to pass. I felt so honored to share in God's work, acting as a vessel through which His love, mercy and compassion could pour out upon those in need. There was no such thing as the "pause" button in God's world after all.

I'll never forget the words of wisdom that came from a woman who waited on God for 40 years until she met her husband. She said, "When I was the only single one left out of my friends, they would all tell me how they were envious of what I had—independence and freedom. Meanwhile, I was envious of what they had—husbands and kids! That's when I realized that no matter where we are in life, the grass only looks greener on the other side. But it's not true. Life is really about being content in whatever season God has us in." She said there were times when she felt lonely and frustrated during her years of being single. But she said she never wanted to look back when she eventually was married, and regret not enjoying that unique time God gave her to be single. So that became her daily prayer—asking God to help her be content, doing all He was asking her to do each day.

When her season of singleness ended, she had no regrets because she had taken full advantage of the time the Lord had given her. She has since been blessed with fourteen years of marriage. Ironically, her prayer for contentment has remained the same, even as a married woman, "Lord, help me be content in this season, doing all you have called me to do today."

God was asking me to be content right then and there with what I had, not confined by what I didn't have. Though there were moments I longed to have someone by my side, I knew He had placed me right there in the season I was living in—anchoring the news by day and serving those young girls every free moment I had—carrying out His Kingdom purposes. In doing that, I discovered a deeply satisfying sweetness in my soul that could only come from being in the perfect will of my Father.

I returned from Manila a changed person. I no longer saw being single as a burden, but a great blessing. This allowed God's power, favor and peace to flow in my daily life. I had desires, yes, but I was no longer trying to win God over to my view of how my life should play out. Rather, I was being won over to His view.

The Bible says no season lasted forever, so I knew the season I was in would eventually end. Like my friend, I wanted to look back without an ounce of regret, knowing that I had fully embraced and fully enjoyed all that He put in front of me. One day at a time.

17

Skype Dates with God

Knowing God is a matter of personal involvement—mind, will and feeling.
It would not indeed be a fully personal relationship otherwise.

~ J. I. Packer

*D*uring the nearly four years I had been living in Asia,
Skype had become my saving grace. It allowed me to stay connected
with friends and family, across oceans and time zones, free of charge.
Since both parties had to be on the computer at the same time, it was
important to set a time and stick to it. There were several times I would
be out doing things, and I would have to leave abruptly. "Sorry guys,
I have a Skype date with my sister!"

It wasn't until one night in Singapore, when I was racing home
to make it on time for one of these sacred Skype sessions, that the Lord
impressed something upon my heart: *His* longing to connect with *me*.
It was as if the Spirit was saying, "You think you could squeeze Me in
for a Skype date?" God wanted me to value connecting with Him as
much as with my loved ones back home.

And that was the beginning of my regular "Skype dates" with God, which would require extended time devoted solely to Him. I was reminded of the verse in the Bible where God's people were instructed to "Be still and know that I am God" (Psalm 46:10). Martin Luther's words reiterated the same point, "Be still and let Him mold you." I wanted to "be still," but it didn't come easily at first. I felt like a kid again, when my sisters and I would get scolded for squirming and bickering in the back seat of the car. My dad would turn around with that stern face that made us tremble, and say "Sit still! I mean it!" For the rest of the drive we remained like statues—stiff, silent and bored.

I felt that same way during my first few sessions with God. Learning to be still took some practice, just like learning anything new, be it a sport, a musical instrument or a new language. It required not only my time, my willingness to learn, and my undivided attention, but also my commitment to show up, even when I didn't feel like it. I had the "doing" part down pat—serving in my church, raising funds for impoverished youth in the Philippines, praying with friends in need. Being active and fully engaged in my community came easy. But sitting still? It was like a thorn in my side—at first.

The time seemed to inch by at a snail's pace those first few sessions with God, as I struggled to overcome my "addiction" to being busy. I struggled to get through ten minutes! But I knew that if I wanted God to continue to mold my character and further direct my steps in every area of my life, then learning the art of being still on a regular basis was a must. Me and Him. Alone. Quiet. Disconnected from the world and connected to His Spirit. Feeling just a glimpse of God's craving to spend time alone, was enough to spur me to make it happen.

One thing that helped the process along was picking a place where God and I could "meet" each morning—a white leather love-seat in my living room, facing the window. Nothing fancy, just a special place for God and me. Then, I would set my alarm one hour before I had to be at work and with my big, fluffy, black robe on I would get comfortable—coffee in hand—and like greeting a friend, "Good morning God, how are you today?"

It was in this Secret Place where God began to teach me the art of being still. One aspect was learning to pour my heart out to Him. In the same way I would share my life with my best friends and family members, God wanted me to share my life with Him. As the psalmist wrote, "Pour out your hearts to Him, for God is our refuge" (Psalm 62:8).

I remember one morning for example, when I felt homesick, wondering when, if ever, I would live closer to my family. A river of tears would flow before God. He didn't shut me up or tell me to toughen up. He just let me let it out. How wonderfully refreshing and safe it was.

I was learning that God's greatest desire was to have this kind of intimate relationship with me, which required constant and consistent communication. I used to think that God knew everything I was thinking and feeling, so there was really no point in expressing it to Him. But it was during those early morning hours that I learned He wanted nothing more than to listen to whatever was on my heart, *Lord, will I ever get married? Lord, will I get to be a mom some day? Lord, what do you want me to do with my life?* Whether I felt sad or discouraged, tired, weary, lost or confused, He was there to hold me in the warmth of His arms and tell me everything was going to be all right.

Pouring my heart out to God was one aspect of being still, but another aspect was listening. God showed me He also had a heart that He wanted to pour out to me. He began to let me in on intimate secrets that were meant only for my own heart and soul. As I simply learned to sit in silence, opening my ears to the heavenly realms, He began to give me words, visions, and directives for my future, directly related to the desires of my heart.

A woman I greatly admired in the faith once said, "I can talk about trust and obedience, and I can teach day and night about the value and beauty it can bring in one's life, but it cannot be forced. It's a message that has to be caught." I was finally catching it. There were even days I wanted to stand on top of the tallest building in Singapore with a giant megaphone, "Everybody listen up... God is REAL! He really is!" I could relate to the psalmist who wrote, "I will declare Your name to My brethren; In the midst of the assembly I will praise you" (Psalm 22:22, NASB). It was hard not to when God was so clearly proving to be the awesome, powerful, loving, sovereign God revealed in the Bible.

As I spent more time with God, He continued to draw me into the deeper side of His heart and plans. It was in this space of uninterrupted time that His Spirit began to express Himself freely, fully and creatively in me. Before I knew it, being still before Him turned from a nagging discipline to a necessity I craved in the early morning hours of each new day.

I realized He wasn't asking me to come to Him in a legalistic or formal way. Nor was He asking me to come to Him as a Martha, busy and bothered. He just wanted me to come, like Mary, to sit at His feet. Raw. Real. Authentic. Just the way I was.

I wrote this prayer out in my journal after one fine morning with God:

> *Lord, thank you that Your presence is more satisfying and more savory than any material thing on this earth. Thank you that I am made whole in Your presence, and am healed of all the wounds that life can bring. Thank you that I can let myself loose in Your arms, finding complete safety for my mind, body and soul. Lord, thank You that You care for me so deeply, and*

You will do anything to bring me into deeper waters with You.
May I pursue You as much as You are pursuing me! Amen.

Pressing "send" on a Skype call up to God's throne, making it a priority to regularly connect with Him each day—whether through worship, prayer, studying His Word, or simply being silent—was the best thing I could have ever done during my "season of singleness." It was in this Secret Place that I received portions of my "daily bread" from Him—whether it was renewed strength, restored hope or wisdom to make choices that were in accordance with His will.

Who said you needed to be in church or at a crusade to experience the mighty things of God? The glory of Heaven was coming to me on a daily basis in my very own living room. All I had to do was show up.

18

Refusing the Pressure Cooker

Transformation happens as you keep company with Jesus...
wanting to keep company with Jesus has a staying power
that 'shoulds' and 'oughts' seldom have.
~ Adele Ahlberg Calhoun

*L*iving in Singapore meant I got to experience many rich cultural traditions and celebrations that were different from my home country. This time it was my first Chinese New Year, so a friend invited me to take part in the festivities with her family.

One of the main traditions was called "visiting," which entailed going to the homes of relatives, greeting them and wishing them a happy and prosperous New Year. I quickly discovered there were some perks to being unmarried during these Chinese celebrations, as I was showered with red packets, or *Ang Pao*. They were filled with money and given only to those who were still "single."

To my surprise though, my friend was less than enthused about the whole deal. "This is the part I dread every year," she said with a sigh.

I couldn't understand how one could possibly dread receiving a gift of money. In fact, I was already scheming in my mind how to introduce this clever tradition to America.

"Well," she explained, "when you're twenty-eight, single and still living at home (which is the norm in Asian culture until you get married), you just get kinda sick and tired of the endless nagging: 'Why aren't you married yet?'"

I may not have been Chinese, but I could relate. It seemed that societal pressures regarding marriage and the age in which it *should* happen were capable of forcing us all, everywhere, into one giant pressure cooker. As a single woman working in the media, questions regarding my relational status were thrown at me all the time. "Not married yet? Why not? How can that be?" Colleagues, taxi drivers, friends and family, you name it. Such questions flew like arrows from all directions.

I say "arrows" because at times they would pierce those deep places in my heart. One day, I had literally been asked by five different people whether I was married or not. Deep down, it was tempting to let fear and doubt creep in: *Why aren't I married yet...is there something wrong with me?*

One particular friend who married in her early forties said, "No matter how much you try, there's no changing God's clock. Just enjoy the season He has you in and rest." I knew that if I wanted to continue living in God's ways, then I would have to surrender my calendar. In other words, I had to throw my time clock out the window. Instead of giving a day or a date, God says, "Everything is made beautiful in its time" (Ecclesiastes 3:11). And that He "...fulfills the desires of those who fear Him..." (Psalm 145:19). If I really believed God's timing was perfect and He would remain true to His promise to fulfill every desire of my heart, what was there to worry about?

I realized ever more the importance of drawing near to God during this season of singleness. Meditating on His Words and dwelling in His presence helped to keep my thoughts, attitudes and perspectives about marriage and His timing rooted in His truth and nothing else. I heeded the instructions given by God to Joshua, "Do not let this Book of the Law depart from your mouth; meditate on it day and night, so that you can be careful to do everything written in it. Then you will be prosperous and successful" (Joshua 1:8). This would protect me from the pressures of the world and preserve my joy and contentment.

As I learned to trust in His promises, I learned to trust ever more in the One who made them. At the end of the day, it wasn't about following a religion, but about having a living relationship with the Creator and lover of my soul. Until it was time to build my life with another person, all the things I wanted to be to that person—a helper, a servant, lover, sister and friend—I could be in my relationship with God.

The questions concerning my marital status didn't stop of course, but instead of getting irritated by them I rejoiced in them. God hadn't called me into marriage yet—so what? It didn't mean I wasn't a whole, complete person capable of living out His purposes! God helped me to see marriage not as a completion of my life and happiness, but as a complement to who I was in Christ.

This revelation really changed the way I saw my so-called status. I felt released from the societal "pressure cooker" paradigm. I wrote out this prayer in my journal.

You, Jesus, are my love, my valentine, my heart's one and only desire! Oh how I long to spend more time getting to know You more intimately, learning how to love You more fully. O dear Jesus, teach me how to honor my commitment to You. You are my safety and my rock and my shield from the arrows of this world. Guard my heart until it's the right time, Your appointed time. Amen.

There would be pressure coming from all different directions, threatening to steal my peace and contentment in God. But it didn't mean I had to give in to it. The next time I was given another Chinese *Ang Pao* to mark my single status, I envisioned Jesus by my side and thought to myself, *If only they knew...I'm not really single.*

19

Awed by His Awesomeness

I praise you because I am fearfully and wonderfully made;
your works are wonderful, I know that full well.

~ Psalm 139:14

One night I went to my Tuesday fellowship group just like any other night. The guest speakers were an American couple from California. At the end of the night the wife shared about a conference she was organizing in Hawaii the following month. It sounded like it would be a great one, but being in Singapore, there seemed to be no way I could go. I really didn't even consider it.

Until my good friend came right up to me after the gathering had ended, "Ali, for some reason I feel like I am supposed to encourage you..." he said, "to go to that conference." In Hawaii? He couldn't be serious. How would I even get the money? The time off work? No, it wasn't possible.

Then came the clincher, "I'll donate my frequent flyer miles to get you a ticket. Just pray about it and give me an answer by the end of the week so I can book the ticket in time."

I agreed and went home a bit dumbfounded. Did God really prompt my friend to tell me that? Or was it just his own idea? Why would He want me to go all the way to Hawaii for a three-day conference anyway?

As I was sitting on the couch in my living room that night, I thumbed through the conference brochure. The verse on the front was Isaiah 60:1, "Arise, shine, for your light has come, and the glory of the Lord rises upon you." I prayed to God, "Lord, if you want me to go to the conference in Hawaii, then please give me a sign."

It was one of those times I was desperately hoping to hear a thundering voice from Heaven, "GO TO THE CONFERENCE, SAYETH THE LORD YOUR GOD." But after a few moments of dead silence, I decided to pick up a book I had been reading the past few weeks. As I flipped to the marked page, the very same verse I had just read from the brochure jumped out, "Arise, shine, for your light has come, and the glory of the Lord rises upon you." The hairs on my arms stood on end as I did a double take, looking back at the book, then the brochure, then the book again. *Could this be?* I wondered, *the sign I just ask God for moments before?*

It may not have been an audible thundering voice, but I chose to believe that seeing that same verse in two different sources, within the span of thirty seconds, was indeed my 'sign' from God telling me to go to the conference. By complete faith, I texted my friend right away and told him, "Well, I got my answer. Book the ticket to Hawaii."

But there were still several details to be worked out. In the back of my mind was this nagging voice of doubt, "I don't think this is really possible." I had heard of these kinds of things happening to *other* people, and I cheered from the sidelines when they did. But I didn't really expect that to happen to me. I was okay with loving God without Him performing some spectacular miracle.

But God seemed to be using this Hawaii incident to readjust my perspective a bit. It was as if He was challenging me head on, "Do you *really* trust in who I am, the Lord your God, who created Heaven and Earth and everything in it?" I was confronted right then and there with a stark realization: my level of trust in God was shaped like a small box and I had put God, and all He was capable of doing, in it. Now, He was saying to me, "Sit back my daughter and watch Me do it."

From that moment all the details started falling into place. My free ticket was booked with my friend's miles and the woman putting on the conference agreed to waive the conference fee, since I was coming all the way from Singapore. And if that wasn't enough, my work schedule just "worked out" without having to take any days off my annual leave count.

Two weeks later I was boarding the plane, on my way to Hawaii. As I was being served a glass of champagne in my Business Class seat, all I could do was whisper a quiet "thank you Father," from a newly humbled heart. I honestly sat there with a renewed sense of awe and wonder of the Lord I served, who was proving to me that through simple faith and obedience, He could carve out any path He wanted to under the sun, unhindered by earthly circumstances.

I was reminded of the verse in Proverbs 1:7, which I had committed to memory months before, but hadn't understood it's true meaning until this moment on the plane. It says, "The fear of the Lord is the beginning of wisdom." I always thought "fear of the Lord" meant I had to tremble before Him in actual nail-biting fear. Though having a healthy fear of God did include a dose of the trembling kind, my soul was being exposed to another kind of fear that saw God with a new sense of awe and reverence. I looked out the window of the plane, knowing that He was the only reason I was on it, and from this high point (literally and metaphorically), I saw a new vision of God's majesty, His greatness, His holiness, His perfect righteousness, His irresistible power, and His sovereign grace. It was this "fear" of Him that would cause me to *want* to walk in His ways with the fullness of my being because I understood the true power and awesome wonder of who He was in relation to His creation. The Bible speaks of this very kind of fear as nothing other than the "foundation of true wisdom" (Psalm 111:10, NLT).

This whole trip I discovered was about God readjusting my view of Him. Through the wonderful women I met at the conference from all over the world, He continued to magnify Himself in powerful ways. I was touched by many of the testimonies shared and inspired by how many women were living fully for the Lord, their faces literally shining radiantly as a result. I kept thinking to myself, *How could I NOT choose to trust this God, who is wonderfully awesome and real?*

The workshops also emphasized God's supernatural ability to make me feel as though he had personally tailored the conference to fit my very own heart. The verses and themes were identical to what He had been teaching me during my quiet times with Him, in the weeks leading up to the conference. God's Spirit was orchestrating it all. Each and every detail. I believed with new conviction the Bible verse that says, "Even the very hairs on your head are numbered" (Matthew, 10:30).

My fear of Him swelled even more as I drank in the majestic beauty of His creation all around me on the tropical island paradise He brought me to. I woke up at five-thirty each morning to watch the sunrise on the beach. I sat alone on the sand, macadamia-nut flavored coffee in hand, listening to the poetic crashing of the waves and my heart was filled with nothing but praises of His awesomeness. I felt a new hope for my future, but this time it wasn't related to Him answering the desires of my heart. It was a hope that said, "I am so grateful to be a part of what You're doing Lord." My soul was laced with a new happiness, awed by a new view of God's majesty.

On the last day of the conference, the leaders prayed and ministered to each person in attendance, encouraging us in our gifts and callings. It was a precious time of rediscovery—not of the plans, hopes, dreams and desires I had in my heart—but of the God who had put them there. I realized much of the time I didn't see myself as God created me to be, because I didn't have a proper understanding of who *He* is. It's like the verse that says, "A plan in the heart of man is like deep water; but a man of understanding draws it out" (Proverbs 20:5). I believe He was turning me into a woman of understanding so that His plans could be drawn out, exposing the very essence of my being.

I suppose the grand finale to this grand adventure I was on with God, came from the prayers of two different women—both of whom didn't know anything about me—at the very end of the last night. The first woman prayed, "I see a key unlocking something. Yes, it's unlocking something that will take you into a new season. New things are up ahead." And the second woman prayed using her gift of prophecy, "The Lord has a husband for you. And a ministry for you both. I see lots of children around you. Together, you will inspire many to come to know the Lord and you will teach them how to walk in His ways."

I remember going back to my seat in the large conference hall, literally shivering in awe. There was no possible way the first woman could have known that the key had been such a relevant image on my journey, except through the Spirit of God. Nor was it humanly possible for the second woman to know that one of my most consistent prayers to God had been to marry someone with a passion for ministry—specifically the children's ministry of which I was a part of in the Philippines. It was as if God was speaking through this woman, "I have heard you Ali, and I will bring it to pass."

But that's not all. I began to see my own desires from a new angle next to God's power and sovereignty. It was no longer solely about me living my life *for* God, but it was about Him manifesting His life *through* me. What a truly awesome privilege.

Going to Hawaii completely blew the lid off the box I had kept God in for so long. This revelation put a new song on my heart that echoed the words of the psalmist who wrote, "I will be glad and exult in you; I will sing praise to your name, O Most High" (Psalm 9:2, ESV). The irony of it all though, was that as I catapulted God back to His rightful position, He simultaneously catapulted me to new levels of faith that made trusting Him not a struggle or a burden, but a gift, wrapped in His abounding love, wisdom and joy.

I returned to Singapore engulfed in fear, but of a holy kind that brought me to my knees, in utter awe of His awesomeness.

PART III

Learning to Wait

*In the morning, O Lord, You hear my voice;
in the morning I lay my requests before You
and wait expectantly.*

~ Psalm 5:3

20

A Good Laugh

…The joy of the Lord is your strength.
~ Nehemiah 8:10

$\mathscr{A}$ few weeks after returning from Hawaii, I flew home to the U.S. from Singapore to visit my family. My twin sister had just given birth to her first child, who was also the first grandchild born amongst my three sisters. We had all arranged to come from our various corners of the world to meet this new little bundle of joy that had entered into the Smith family.

When I boarded the plane I was pleased to see that my seat was in the Exit Row, giving me a little more leg room for the nearly 24-hour journey. As I was buckling my seatbelt, another bonus awaited me: a handsome man across the aisle. It was *him*, the man I had already noticed in the ticket line at the airport. I was both glad and annoyed, as I knew this would probably occupy my thoughts for the rest of the ride: *Should I say something? Should I not? Do I look okay?* Etc…

It's both fascinating and funny to me how the female mind can run wild. For example, within minutes of seeing this man (not even meeting him), I had already imagined what a great "how we met" story this would make. "We were both flying back to the U.S. and were seated next to each other...and well, it was love at first sight!" I honestly had to put the brakes on my thoughts, or else they would run way ahead of me, and God.

As the plane took off, I decided to use the time to take this to bring this situation to the beholder of my heart's key in my journal,

> *Lord, there's a funny thing going on here on this plane. There's a man seated right across from me. Slightly older, but handsome. Tall. Blonde-haired. Blue eyed. You see him. Oh wait, You created him. Ha! I am asking You to tell me whether you are in on this. A few questions:*
>
>> *Who is this guy?*
>> *Does he know You?*
>> *Is there a reason why we are seated next to each other?*
>> *Would You like us to exchange words?*
>
>> *Lord, You know I am curious by nature, so this is killing me. But I only want what You want...is there ANY chance this could be what You want ?!*

I realized that God was probably laughing at me, as I divulged my every thought to Him. I was laughing with Him, too, knowing full well that ultimately He was the one who knew how it would all pan out.

I loved that I could share with God even my silliest, most random thoughts. He was there to listen and give comfort and guidance along the way, as a best friend would. I felt free to joke with God, confident that He knew my heart and everything in it.

We finally landed in Tokyo. As I walked off the plane, this mysterious man asked where I was headed. After all, we were the only Caucasians on the flight. We chatted as we waited in the security line to get to our connecting gates. During this time, I found out that he had been married and divorced. Two kids. Girlfriend. Not a Christian. Worked for a beer company. A very nice man indeed, but it ended there.

God wanted me not only to let Him be my Shepherd, leading me in all things, but He wanted me to enjoy it too. He wanted me to come to Him for guidance and instruction, but He had a treasure chest of other blessings too like rest, relaxation and enjoyment. I wrote out this prayer to God,

> *Dear Lord, I am sorry for wanting to rush through life, hurrying from one thing to the next. Help me to slow down and enjoy what you have put before me, fully living in each moment. As I do this, restore my soul and help me wait patiently for Your will to come to pass. Amen.*

After we made it through the security line, the man on the plane and I parted ways. *Oh well*, I thought, as I waited to board the next leg of my journey back to the U.S., *thanks for the laugh God*. Sometimes, it just felt good to let loose and have a good laugh with God.

21

Staying on the Potter's Wheel

"God sees in us a masterpiece that one day will be done;
His Spirit works throughout our lives to make us like His son."

- Sper

I was visiting my twin sister Kelli and her husband Aaron in Maine, along with their newborn baby, Abe. It was such a joy seeing my sister in her new roles as wife and mother. I could see how God had molded her over the years, as a potter would his clay. All of the "rough edges" that were there during our childhood days had seemingly been smoothened as she took on her new duties.

Admittedly, though, it was also a bit strange seeing my sister so "grown up"—a sort of reality check that we had arrived at an age where childbearing and motherhood were becoming the norm. I didn't know whether to rejoice in that fact or freak out all together.

It seemed like just days ago when we had been in the 5th grade, chasing boys together on the playground. Fast forward 15 years. Now I sat holding my baby nephew in the early morning hours, bearing witness to the drastically different ways and paces at which our love adventures had evolved. Here she was with a husband, a house, two dogs and a child. And there I was with...well, none of those things.

I wondered how the years ahead would continue to mold and shape her as a wife and mother, but also as a child of God. I wondered too how my own love adventure would morph and meander with time. When would I be holding a child of my own? Would I be ready to take on the kind of responsibilities that came along with marriage and having children?

As twins, we had been compared to one another our entire life. No matter how old we got, there continued to be comparisons. In this phase of life, it was people saying, "Ali, when are you going to settle down like your sister?" Or "Is it tough being single when your sister is already married?" Just because we entered into the world at the same time, it was somehow expected that we enter into life's different stages at the same time too.

My sister and I were indeed living out the scripts of two different screenplays. But I believed God had His reasons for the seasons that were unfolding one scene at a time. I lifted all these thoughts up to God and asked Him to prepare both my sister and me for our respective seasons yet to come, and for both of us to enjoy the current one we were in.

God reminded me that He was the potter and I was his blob of clay, ready and willing to be molded and shaped, according to His will. He would smoothen out every bump and add water to any dry, cracked edges. All I had to do was stay right where he had me—on His wheel—until His hands had finished their work.

22

Not Every Man You Meet is a Potential Mate

Christ has no body now on earth but yours,
no hands but yours, no feet but yours.

~ Teresa Avila

My family was completely smitten with our nephew in Maine. One evening we were planning to have a barbeque at my sister's home so we could meet some of their friends. Little did we know we were in for an unexpected adventure.

My sister, mom, brother-in-law and I entered the grocery store to shop for the evening cookout. Suddenly, my attention was drawn to a very tall and handsome male specimen shopping in the row next to us. Apparently, my mom and sister noticed him too. They were nudging me in the side, giving me "the look" as if to say, "He's cuuuuute!"

Since I was the only single person in the group, everyone seemed determined to play matchmaker—even in grocery stores. I appreciated the gesture, but let's be serious. Too much of this can make a person feel like one big charity case.

Meanwhile, the scene at the store only continued to get more comical. As we passed one row, he passed by on the opposite end. By that time, it was clear he had noticed us too. Who knows what he was thinking, but the awkwardness was escalating by the minute.

Finally, we approached the produce section, where he also happened to be. It was too late to turn back, or it would have looked like we were intentionally avoiding him. So we continued to walk towards him. This time, I poked my mom in the side, murmuring (more like pleading) under my breath, "Say something, say something, say something!" We were at the point of no return. Someone *had* to say something. He turned around, and suddenly my 54-year-old mother blurted out, "Uh hi there, are you from Portland?"

He looked quite shocked. I don't think he had thought we had the nerve to actually say something. He mumbled nervously, "Um, I work here in Portland, but I am not originally from here."

That's how the conversation started. It ended with my sister's invitation to the barbeque that night at her house, which he accepted. "Okay, see you tonight!" He paid for his groceries and left.

A daze came over me as I realized what had just transpired. My very own mom had successfully picked up the cute guy in the grocery store. I wanted to crawl under a rock to hide my shame! If I had known surrendering the key to my heart meant I was going to be reduced to such a pathetic case, I might have reconsidered altogether.

All kidding aside, I was actually looking forward to finding out more about this guy. All I knew about him so far was that he shopped in the produce section. *A good sign*, I thought, *it obviously indicates healthy eating habits.* I didn't even know him and he was already earning brownie points in my imaginary book of "future husband" traits.

This threw a totally unexpected loop into the Smith family vacation. I wondered once again if this was someone God wanted me to meet or if it was a mere coincidence. As we drove home, I prayed silently, "Lord, are you in on this? Please show me Your will and may it be done."

The rest of the afternoon seemed to inch by. I had to keep my thoughts from racing way ahead of myself and God. It was so tempting to try to figure out God's plans ahead of time. *Maybe this time he'll be 'the one'...maybe this will be the story I'll share to all my friends...tonight could be my last night of being single.* It may sound crazy, but that's honestly where my mind would wander if I let it.

I felt like a school girl again, crushing on a boy I liked. Those familiar "butterflies" were fluttering around in my stomach, something I hadn't felt in a long time. I felt free to let my heart feel, though. I realized that sometimes I had been so careful to "guard my heart" that this became synonymous with "disengaging" it altogether. Though there were times when God had asked me to refrain from engaging with a person, it was not a hard rule. There wasn't anything inherently wrong with having a natural excitement about meeting someone new. What was important was taking these feelings to God and asking Him to help me manage them in a way that pleased Him. He was giving me the freedom to flow with these natural feelings, while *He* would be the one to protect and guard my heart.

I spent some time before the barbeque alone with God, reading His Word and letting it direct my thoughts back to Him. I wrote out this prayer in my journal.

> *God, I pray you help me keep these feelings at bay as I approach the evening. Thank You for the opportunity to get to know someone new. Help steer my thoughts and conversations in ways that are pleasing to You. Help me to see into this person's*

life and character. I only desire to do what You tell me to do Lord. Help me and be with me tonight! I love You.

Over the course of the evening, I learned a lot of things about this guy. First, he was really brave to come over to spend an evening with my entire family. Secondly, he made a killer mango salsa! Did I mention he played the guitar, cooked, was a former athlete, and spoke fondly of his family? On paper, he would be described by most women's standards as an "ideal prospect."

I was impressed by his lengthy list of talents, hobbies and accomplishments, but I was already looking beyond these things, into his heart. I was searching for any clue that might indicate some value system or belief in God. A cross hanging around his neck? Perhaps a reference to church? Or maybe standing on the table and screaming at the top of his lungs, "I LOVE JESUS!!" would do the trick. Okay, that might have been a little extreme. But it seemed to me that if he was a man after God's own heart, he would have been curious to know where I stood too.

It wasn't until we were sent to the store for hotdog buns that I discovered the clue I had been looking for all night long. He had a small tattoo on his forearm that read "*Faith*." My heart did a cartwheel. Actually it was more like a triple flip. *This could be it,* I thought. *Perhaps this is the "sign" God is giving me.*

I debated whether to inquire myself or wait for him to bring it up. I couldn't hold back. "Do you mind if I ask what your tattoo means?" I waited with bated breath for him to launch into a passionate sermon about his love for God.

"Well..." Hesitation. Long pause. And then finally, "This is the name of my baby daughter...who passed away." Oh man, I felt horrible. Here I was, totally consumed in my own thoughts, running through the checklist of reasons why he was or wasn't a good match for me. And there he was trying to put words to a recent tragedy in his life.

I felt like I had been punched in the side, convicted of my own selfishness. God had put this man in my life for a reason, but it wasn't to marry him. Far from it. This person was lost and hurting, trying to make sense of his sudden loss. He did not know God, but he was open to learning about Him. I was thankful for the opportunity to share about my faith in Jesus and how the love of God had transformed my life.

I got on my knees that night to pray. Not only to ask forgiveness from my Father, but to pray for my new grocery store friend—that he would somehow come to know the great, powerful and unconditional love of God one day and that he would again meet his beautiful daughter in Heaven.

God used this situation to gently remind me of something very important: it wasn't always about me. I had somehow adopted a one-track mind with each new male that stepped onto my path, *Is he a potential mate?* Instead, I need to see each person as a child of God, and my initial desire should be to show this person God's love.

I went to bed that night resting in my Father's arms with peace in my heart. No, the cute grocery store guy didn't turn out to be "the one" God picked out for me after all. But He had picked *me* out to share a bit of His love to someone who needed it. And for that I was thankful.

23

Serendipity

…I have summoned you by name, you are mine.
~ Isaiah 43:1

$\mathcal{I}$was furiously typing away on my laptop when the flight attendant came over the intercom. "Final boarding call for flight number 4471 to Singapore, final call." I was on my way back to Singapore from the U.S. after a wonderful trip visiting my family. I had some time to kill, so I thought I would catch up on some emails (why did airports have to get wireless?). I quickly typed the last sentence to a friend and pressed "send" and began to frantically pack up my things.

That's when I noticed him, another very handsome young man sitting right next to me. I reminded myself of what I had just learned and decided it was a perfect opportunity to put it into practice, *Okay, child of God first, Ali. Potential husband material, second.* This trip had been so peculiar, in that for some reason I was taking notice of the men around me. This "heightened awareness" was not the norm.

This time, the person of interest wasn't across the row on the plane, like on my way to the U.S. Nor was he strolling the aisle next to me in the grocery store, like in Maine. He was two chairs over—close enough to smell the hazelnut flavor steaming from his Starbucks coffee. I had been so consumed with my computer; I hadn't even noticed him sit down. I wanted to stand there and stare, but instead I did the opposite: pretended I didn't notice him and ran away (literally) to board the plane.

As I handed my ticket to the agent at the door, I took one last look in his direction. I made sure to play it cool, though—not wanting to look too obvious. I pretended I was making sure I didn't leave any belongings behind. The thought crossed my mind as I pulled my ticket from my bag, *Should I go back and introduce myself?* But I chickened out. I walked through the door, boarded the plane and was on my way.

I sat on the plane trying to read my book, but I struggled to control my thoughts. It was as if there was a wrestling match going on in my heart and I didn't even know who the opponents were. So I set down my book and attempted to think through what had just happened. I couldn't help but wonder if maybe I was supposed to talk to that guy, but missed the opportunity. I even asked God straight up, *Lord, did I mess up your plan?*

I was reminded of the romantic comedy called *Serendipity,* starring John Cusack and Kate Beckinsale. The one that makes you want to scream because the two lovers—who had met one random night and left it up to "fate" to connect them back together—keep missing each other by a split second. Just when they are about to meet, one of them gets distracted or pulled in the other direction. Their timing is just off by a hair.

I sat there on the plane wondering if the same thing was possible in God's world. Could I accidentally miss God's plans, by a hair? After all, He gives us a free will to make our own decisions. Maybe if I had stopped emailing just a few minutes before, then perhaps we could have had a chance to strike up a conversation. Or what if I hadn't even been emailing in the first place and was reading a book instead? Then I definitely would have noticed him sitting next to me. A sinking feeling in the pit of my stomach seemed to be saying, *Ali, you missed it.*

But just as I was imagining the conversation I "might have had" with this complete stranger, God interrupted, breathing a verse from His Word into my spirit, "Before I formed you in the womb, I knew you..." from Jeremiah 1:5. It was all I needed to bring me back to reality—His reality. I let out a sigh of relief as I felt the strength and providence of my Creator's embrace. He had every single step of my life worked out. He had a hope and a future for me,[10] independent of serendipitous luck or accidental fate. He had already gone ahead of me and prepared the way.

This didn't mean there would be no consequences for the actions I chose. But as long as I continued to choose His path, earnestly seeking to honor Him with my life, I could be sure that He wouldn't let me "miss" His plan.

I spent the rest of the plane ride digging up other precious jewels from God's Word. I was learning that Scripture was really the only thing with the staying power to keep my thoughts on track, especially when dealing with matters of my heart. Otherwise, the messages of the world could creep into my thoughts, threatening to steal the very peace and joy that God desires me to have in knowing Him.

One verse that particularly grabbed me during that flight was, "...The Lord will again delight in you and make you prosperous, just as he delighted in your fathers" (Deuteronomy 30:9). The thought of

God rejoicing over my good with all His heart and all His soul sent soothing chills down my spine. I imagined God himself hovering above me belting out in a boisterous singing voice, *"Ali my beloooooooved, my valentine...oh if you only knew....how much I love you...sweet child of mine!"* It doesn't do it justice to write it out, but I really was imagining God bursting forth in song as I sat nibbling airplane peanuts. I suddenly had the feeling that I could sit there on that plane for the rest of my life, doing absolutely nothing, and He would still be rejoicing over little old me. Wow.

I got off the plane, marching once again to the beat of God's drum. It was hard not to after He had serenaded me all the way home. I knew that if I continued to delight in Him and He continued to delight in me, there was no such thing as serendipity.

24

Lonely but Not Alone

An enormous loneliness emerges, but you are not frightened.
You feel vulnerable but safe at the same time. Jesus is where you are,
and you can trust he will show you the way.

~ Henri Nouwen

Returning to life in Asia from the U.S. was always a transition. This time, the transitional period entailed unusual waves of loneliness and sadness. I had gotten used to being around my family again. Going back to being worlds apart from them left a deep void in my heart.

I noticed myself releasing sighs from deep within, the kind of sighs that made me pause for a moment, thinking, *Where is that coming from?* I would try to rationalize them, "Maybe it's my odd work schedule," or explain them away, "I'm probably just tired from the long flight." But I knew there was something more going on deep down inside, though I couldn't exactly put my finger on it.

I sat alone in Starbucks one day, and it suddenly felt like I was attacked by a flock of love birds. In every direction there were couples—walking hand in hand, strolling the mall, laughing, kissing, and just being together. I felt like pulling out a giant megaphone, and standing on the table to make an announcement: "ATTENTION ALL LOVERS: please withhold any form of physical affection or else leave the premises. Thank you."

I pretended to be disgusted, but deep down I wondered if that would ever be me—with someone else. Who would he be? When and where would we meet? Would my family get to be a part of it? When would it be time to awaken my heart's desires? Yearning and burning, they were like a hot fire deep within my soul.

It was at this moment when I felt the Lord saying, "Ali, it's okay to *not* feel okay all the time." I realized that somewhere along the line, I had adopted a notion that having a strong relationship with the Lord meant I had to feel happy all the time. But such a state was unnatural and would require a manipulation of the real emotions I was feeling. I was reminded of Jesus, whose life's journey on earth entailed times of anguish, anger, weeping and crying out to God.[11] He was recorded in the gospel of John as saying, "Now is my soul troubled. And what shall I say? 'Father, save me from this hour'? But for this purpose I have come to this hour" (John 12:27, ESV). Even Jesus, the son of God, experienced valleys of emotion while He waited for God's purposes to unfold in their proper time.

I felt the Holy Spirit encouraging me to pour out my heart to Him right then and there. It was as if God was lifting me into His lap and saying, "My child, tell me what is troubling your heart." I wrote the following conversation with God in my journal:

> *Abba, I feel tired of waiting today. I know your timing is perfect but when will it be Lord? I feel ready to share my life*

with someone...my heart...my dreams...my body...to build a life together...raise a family together...serve You together...oh Lord, who will it be? Where will we live out our life? How long must I wait for the appointed time to come, oh Lord?

Search my heart, mind and soul this moment Father. Dive into the depth of my being. Am I holy before You right now? Am I whole enough to be with someone else? Am I ready to give of myself? Am I ready to receive someone else? Are my thoughts and attitudes pleasing to You, Abba?

Even as I lift up all these questions and burning desires up to You God, thank You that I have such a peace in my spirit. A quiet confidence that You won't leave me to shrivel up into an old woman. I choose to believe that You have awesome plans for my husband and me—as individuals and as a couple, a spiritual unit bound by Your love. I believe You are going to do mighty things through us for Your glory.

Give me the patience to WAIT on you Lord, my Abba Father. Patience! Oh I am so eager, expectant, excited for this desire of my heart to be fulfilled.

Until then, please be with me when I feel lonely. Remind me that I am never alone. Be with me as I endure and persevere through moments of long-suffering. When will it end?? My soul cries out to You my Lord, my Savior, my Father and best friend in the whole world!

Thank you for how You are preparing me right now for the next season to come, even as I sit here alone in Starbucks. Thank you for who You are Lord and for how You are at work, always for the good of your children who love You. O how I love you so, even when my heart hurts from waiting. Amen.

I was learning that during these moments of "long-suffering," God did not expect me to suppress my emotions, but to express them—to Him. I found the Book of Psalms to be a great place to help me be able to express the eager yearnings and longings, both for God's presence and His promises to come to pass. Every emotion known to man—from joy, praise, and trust to repentance, anguish and doubt—flowed from the human hearts of David and the other Psalmists. A few verses that gave voice to my waiting heart during the more difficult times were:

"My soul is in anguish. How long, O LORD, how long?"
~ Psalm 6:3

"Hear my prayer, O LORD, and give ear to my cry;
Do not be silent at my tears..."
~ Psalm 39:12 (NASB)

"Relieve my troubled heart, and bring me out of my distress."
~ Psalm 25:17 (GWT)

"Wait calmly for God alone,
my soul, because my hope comes from him."
~ Psalm 62:5 (GWT)

Giving expression to my longings and emotions was necessary at times, but it didn't mean I was to dwell in that place for too long. He didn't want me to focus so much on the "destination," or what I was waiting for, that I forgot to enjoy the ride. Though the end result of His promise was important—whether it was a promotion, a house, a husband or child—so was the means of getting there.

My twin sister, who had recently entered into motherhood, said to me, "Ali, take advantage of the time and independence you have while you're single, because never again will you have it the same way!" She was right. There were special blessings to be found in each season God had us in. It didn't mean I had to run around jumping for joy that I was single. But I could give thanks to God even when I didn't feel thankful. The Apostle Paul instructed the church on this point, telling them to "Be joyful always; pray continually; give thanks in all circumstances, for this is God's will for you in Christ Jesus" (1 Thessalonians 5:16-18).

Giving thanks to God was not always an expression of emotion—but an act of will. It meant choosing to believe that God had allowed my circumstances and had a reason and ultimately a good purpose for the season I was in. Choosing to give thanks for the blessings rather than complain about the "lack" of them in my life would bring His joy, peace and hope.

On days when I just wasn't "feeling the joy," I started the habit of "willing it," by writing down the special blessings I was thankful for that day in my journal.

Thank you Lord for...

> ♣ *The close friends you have blessed me with*
> ♣ *My night work schedule so I can have more time with you in the mornings*
> ♣ *The desire and enthusiasm you have given me to write*
> ♣ *For the special gift of being able to travel to different places*

There were times that called for expression of the deep and overwhelming longings of my soul. But I knew that even when I was feeling down in the dumps, I could choose to wait on God, trusting that His hope would be around the corner, "...they who wait for the Lord shall renew their strength; they shall mount up with wings like eagles; they shall run and not be weary; and they shall walk and not faint" (Isaiah 40:31, ESV).

There would be some rough terrain on my earthly road, bringing moments of pain and suffering. But God would never require an artificial display of emotion. All He wanted was my faith and my trust that He would bring me through.

I left Starbucks that day letting out another deep sigh, but this time it was one of great relief. No matter how low or lonely I felt, I was never truly alone.

25

Total Life-Sharing Intimacy

We long for moments of expressions of love, closeness and tenderness,
but frequently, at the critical point, we often draw back.
We are afraid of closeness. We are afraid of love.

~ Marshall Hodge, *Your Fear of Love*

I rounded the last corner. The end was in sight. All the months of training for my half marathon had led up to *this* moment. As I crossed the finish line, I heard a familiar voice in the crowd, "Go Ali go, go Ali go!" It was my dear friend and housemate at the time, Kate. I was shocked to see her because I had told her "not to bother." I didn't want her to waste a morning coming to watch *me* race—how boring! But there she was, all smiles and cheers, loaded with the best "after-race" remedies like Gatorade, sliced oranges, a power bar, and a camera to capture my moment of triumph.

Kate showing up to support me in my race that day exposed a super independent lifestyle I had adopted over the years—which God never intended me to have. I had gotten used to going about things on my own, not relying on anyone for anything. People like Kate would try to enter my life, and I would say, "Don't bother."

No wonder God was giving me a wake-up call. My lifestyle was conveying an attitude that was the complete opposite of what He intended. He created us to have not independent, but interdependent intimate relationships with Him and one another. I was living and breathing independence, defined as "exemption from reliance on others; self-subsistence or maintenance; direction of one's own affairs without interference,"[12] while the Bible says, "...if we walk in the light, God himself being the light, we also experience a *shared life* with one another..." (1 John 1:7, MSG)

This opened my eyes to see that my relationship with God meant that I would, or should, experience a "shared life" with the people around me. On the surface, I was sharing my life with lots of different people. I was plugged into my church community. I would go to different social events and ministry gatherings. But if I were to go around and ask them how much they actually knew about the *real* me, they probably wouldn't have much to say beyond the basic facts: newscaster from Montana who ran marathons. Though it had appeared I was "sharing my life" with many, I wasn't really sharing it with anyone.

With God, it wasn't a numbers game. He was much more concerned about quality than quantity when it came to relationships. His greatest desire was to have deep and meaningful fellowship with His children and therefore, expected me to mirror that same Kingdom characteristic of intimacy on earth.

If God wanted me to emulate intimacy, I had to know exactly what it meant. The word is usually used in reference to the marriage relationship or our relationship with God. But the literal meaning of the word, "total life sharing," enlightened my perspective. All God's children are called to share their life totally with each other.

I had learned this kind of closeness with God over the previous three years. I had no problem sharing my inner life with God. I knew He would always love me no matter what. I could be open, vulnerable and weak in His presence, and His love for me would never change. But what would it mean to share my life totally with my friends? The thought was terrifying. There was risk involved in getting close to someone and allowing them to step inside my personal boundaries. I was scared of what they might think of me.

God presented me with a prime opportunity to begin practicing this "total life-sharing" intimacy the weekend following the race. I went with Kate and another dear friend, Kelsey, for a "mini getaway" at a beach in Indonesia. What was supposed to be a weekend of fun in the sun turned into a soul-filled sharing saga, in a good way. Our hopes, fears, struggles and insecurities flowed openly and freely in a raw and beautiful way. My fear of rejection slowly melted away, and we embraced each other with open arms. The guard I had unknowingly built up around my heart was coming down. For the first time, I was letting someone, besides God, have a look at the inner sanctuary of my soul. It wasn't so scary after all.

As we rode the ferry back to Singapore, God put something on my heart: learning a new level of intimacy with my friends was part of preparing my heart for the kind of intimate relationship He intended me to share within a marriage one day. Minus, of course, a few things. But it would be this kind of intimacy, or ability of sharing myself totally with a mate, that would birth the fruits of joy, satisfaction and fulfillment God intended us to have.

This is a prayer I wrote out in my journal during the weekend retreat with my girlfriends.

> *Dear Lord, thank You for placing soul sisters in my path, with whom I can share this life journey. Thank You*

for teaching me about the sweet intimacy that You intend for relationships—with You and with others. Lord, thank you for showing me that my friends will love me unconditionally, no matter what. Continue to remove my fears of judgment and rejection. Thank you that through this You are preparing me to be a godly wife who will know how to share my life totally and completely. Thank You that as a result, I will share a joyfully rich and intimate relationship with my husband that is bound by our intimacy with You. Amen.

I was thankful God gifted me with certain friends during the season of being single to start learning the ropes of intimacy—before I entered into marriage. Not just friends with whom I could go out and have a good time, although those were important too. I'm talking about "soul-level" friendships like Kate and Kelsey, that sought to build each other up in our godly character, pray and encourage each other in our faith and would help reveal aspects of our hearts that weren't yet fully functioning the way God intended.

Learning to be vulnerable and letting others into my life was scary and uncomfortable at times. But I had the sense that this entire process was so God could answer a prayer that was near and dear to my heart: to have a godly marriage that would glorify His Name. I couldn't think of one reason why God *wouldn't* want to answer that prayer.

I was ready to share my life with someone fully, totally and completely.

26.

A Lesson on Yokes

For we are God's workmanship, created in Christ Jesus to do good works,
which God prepared in advance for us to do.

~ Ephesians 2:10

One day, a friend of mine shared about an elderly woman she
had met in Japan while on a mission trip. The woman came up to my
friend and tearfully said, "I admire so much that you are obeying your
call to the mission field. The Lord put missions on my heart over 30
years ago, when I was about your age. But when I met and married my
husband, he was not called to missions, so I had to put it aside."

This story made me feel sad, though I couldn't immediately
pinpoint why. It set me thinking about my life's "calling" (which I was
still in the process of discovering) and how God intended it to gel with
a mate. Though I knew there would be times God would ask me to set
certain things aside for the sake of unity in a marriage, I also wanted
to believe there was a purpose behind the dreams he had been putting
on my heart. One of my heart's deepest longings, for example, was to
minister internationally with my husband. I believed He had placed
this in my heart to be lived out in marriage, not squelched by it.

reminded me of Paul's instruction to the Corinthian church … not be yoked together with unbelievers" (2 Corinthians 6:14). This passage has generated much discussion in the church, in regards to what exactly Paul meant by "unbelievers." But hearing the story of the Japanese woman, it seemed that being "equally yoked" went beyond sharing faith, to include matters like life calling and purpose. David Lipscomb, in his commentary on Paul's second epistle to the Corinthians, wrote, "To be unequally yoked would be to be…persons that do not harmonize in purpose, walk, and life."[13]

A simple Google search helped me to dig deeper into the meaning of "yokes." During Moses's time, farmers would use an "equal yoke" to plow their fields. Two animals of the same kind would be "yoked together" according to equal strength and ability, making the plowing as easy and as straight as possible. If a large horse and a small goat were yoked together, for example, it would be highly unlikely that the farmer could plow a straight line. One member would overpower the other, with negative results.[14]

The agricultural metaphor was making sense, despite the fact that I was living in one of the most urbanized cities in Asia. Choosing to marry someone with a completely different calling in life would in a way be a selfish decision. I would be the goat, putting strain on the yoke of the horse as he attempted to plow through life the way God intended him to. It's not to say it could never work, but it might make it more difficult and less enjoyable than necessary. God helped to bring further clarity to this principle in a real life situation.

It began with a simple "friend invite" on Facebook. Even though I had a sort of love-hate relationship with the whole social networking thing, I would usually succumb to any invite requests I received through email from people whose names I at least recognized.

I had met this particular man the day before, in church. He had been invited to be a guest singer with our worship team—all the way from Israel. As an African American, fully decked out in dreadlocks, a cloak, and a Jewish *kippah*, or skullcap (traditionally worn by observant Jews), he stuck out like a sore thumb among our Asian Protestant congregation.

His unique look paralleled His music. His songs were a mixture of Hebrew and English, many of them derived from the Psalms in the Bible. The melodies sounded ancient and foreign, and yet they sparked an odd familiarity in the souls of those of us listening.

There I sat the next day, staring at my computer screen wondering if our brief encounter the day before (we had met briefly after the service) was enough to warrant the "Accept" button. *Oh, what the heck*, I thought, as I moved my arrow to click the little green box. That's when I saw a message asking if I would like to meet him for coffee before he flew back to Jerusalem the following week.

The same curiosity that killed the cat was killing me. Something intrigued me about this peculiar psalmist and I wanted to know more. Besides, he was explicit in stating that he was "seeking friendship." We set a time to meet the following day.

Conversation was rich and enjoyable. He had an inspiring testimony of being born in Haiti and living as an aspiring musician in New York City, before the Lord called him to Jerusalem. We shared a common love for Jesus (*Yeshua*, as he called Him) and a desire to live out God's call over our lives. I was enthralled by His sharp ability to hear God and his willingness to obey, whatever the cost. He didn't take himself too seriously, though. We spent half the time laughing and joking.

I went home not knowing what to think. I had enjoyed the company of this new friend—this Jesus-loving Jewish Psalmist, who yes, was also single. He was a unique find, for sure. In a moment of emotional bewilderment, I wrote this prayer in my journal.

> *Hi God, thank You for the enjoyable fellowship with a new friend today. Thank You Lord for his love for You that shines radiantly upon his face. It is apparent Your Spirit is living in and through Him and I am grateful for the opportunity to have encountered such a unique soul on my road. Lord, I ask that you make known Your purpose for our meeting. Shall we meet again? He is so totally not anyone I could ever imagine engaging with beyond a level of friendship, but Lord I don't want to just cut him off for that reason. Help me keep an open mind and please give me a wise and discerning heart Lord. Thank you. Amen.*

A few days later, this new friend invited me for dinner at the home of his host family. It was possible that his original intention of only "seeking friendship" had changed. I had enjoyed myself, but I didn't want to give him the wrong idea, leading him to think I was "interested."

I consulted my trusted girlfriend Kelsey about whether to go to the dinner. She had the perfect solution: "Why don't I come with you?" I accepted her offer and brought her along to help read the situation and ease any potential awkwardness. Every girl needed a wing-woman, right? Or perhaps "wing-sister" is a more suitable name.

We arrived at the home of the host family, and immediately it became clear: he was definitely interested. The entire family was standing around like a pack of eager beavers, as if they had been waiting all day to meet "the girl" their guest had been talking about. My wing-sister also took notice of the little things that gave him away. According to her, it was the way he looked at me and the way in which he was trying to impress—basically, the normal things guys do when they like someone.

Despite the initial awkwardness, however, we did manage to have a nice dinner. This man's passion for God continued to come through as he told us about his life in Jerusalem. He was a compelling story teller who captured the interest of us all. Not to mention, he pulled out his guitar and serenaded us as dessert was being served!

I would be lying if I said I didn't, for a moment, consider what it would be like jumping onboard the specific calling over his life—to minister to the Jewish community in Jerusalem. We were both passionate believers seeking to live out His will. But after another moment's thought I just couldn't see myself in his picture for the long term. I would have been an "unequal yoke," or the small goat, making it more difficult than necessary for him to plow, probably resulting in a crooked line rather than a straight one in God's kingdom field. What a shame that would be!

I wrote out this prayer in my journal that night after the dinner.

> *Dear Lord, thank you for your faithfulness. You are never a second too early or late in delivering Your wisdom, clarity and revelation. I have a completely new and deeper understanding of what it means to be equally yoked now. Father, I pray that you will give me the strength to be patient to marry someone, not just who believes in You, but also someone who follows You and is headed in the same direction. Lord. I ask that You bless my Jewish friend with an equal yoke, who can support him in His calling. I ask that you bless me also with someone next to whom I can plow side by side, making a perfectly straight line in Your glorious kingdom field. Amen.*

I had a deep peace about remaining friends with this person. My wing-sister also confirmed this. She saw a match in terms of spiritual passion and maturity, but she did not see our life paths going in the same direction. And just in case I needed convincing (and some humor!); she sent me the following in an email that read: "This could be you in Jerusalem in ten years...."

I got the point.

This situation further clarified my understanding of why God instructs us to be equally yoked in marriage. His desire is for us to walk out fully His beautiful plans over our lives, which practically speaking, is easier to do when two people are of equal strength and united in purpose. This didn't mean it was necessary to share identical life "callings" in order to come together as a couple. But I did believe that as a wife, I would play a supporting role to whatever call the Lord put on my husband's heart. So whatever that turned out to be—no matter how similar to mine or how different from it—I would have to be willing to jump on board, trusting that my gifts and callings would somehow gel or compliment him in a way that only God knew.

Whenever I met someone new, I realized the importance of asking some of the "big picture" questions like: In which direction will my life go if I spend my life with this person? Is this in line with God's vision and calling on my life? Can I see myself jumping onto his passions and dreams? What is the Lord asking me to put aside, and what is He asking me to hold on to?

God seemed to be telling me in all of this, "Hold fast, Ali, to the calling I have for you *and* your husband." Though I didn't know what it would look like or who he would be, I did know one thing: we would be equally yoked together, plowing a straight line through God's glorious field.

27

Signs or Insanity?

Faith looks across the storm—it does not doubt or stop to look at
things without. Faith does not question why when all His ways are
hard to understand, but trusts... and prays.

~ Anonymous

he same week I bid farewell to my Messianic Jewish friend,
a new person appeared on my heart's radar screen. Well, he actually
first appeared on my computer screen after a friend emailed an article
with a message, "How are you going to get this guy involved in your
Philippines ministry?"

I didn't know what he meant until I read in the New York Times
article. This man had been born to American missionary parents in the
Philippines and though he no longer lived there, he and his parents and
siblings continued to run an orphanage and do mission work there.
Not only that, he was known as a successful athlete in the U.S. who
spoke openly about his faith in Christ and his passion to bring hope
to the poor.

My heart seemed to be doing backflips and aerials as I skimmed
the article. The uncanny similarities made every hair on my arms stand

on end. *Passionate believer and follower of Christ... American with special connection to the Philippines...involvement in Prison Ministry...Sports.* It was as if God was saying, "Here you go, Ali—all you have ever dreamed of in a life partner." I remember sitting at my desk at work that day I read the article, my heart and mind racing with possibility as I imagined being "yoked" together with such a person.

Then, the whistling bell of the afternoon snack cart in my office jolted me back to reality: he was in America, I was in Asia—do the math. The impossibility of the situation was staring me right in the face. This person had no clue of my existence, and I had no clue if he ever would. The only thing to do was give it over to God, which I proceeded to do in this letter to Him.

> *Lord, are you up to something? Are you drawing my attention to this man? Or is this just coincidence? The man written about in the article has captured my heart like no one else. I confess to you that my heart is excited by the possibilities: potential ministry, potential friends who share the same heart for this corner of the world, potential "life partner." O Lord, I am so curious to see how you will unravel this mystery!*
>
> *Just by reading about this person's life, testimony and future dreams to influence others through Christ, is without a doubt, in line with the prayers that I know You have heard from my heart. I pray Lord Jesus, that if it is Your will that this man and I meet, then let it be done. It's going to have to be a miracle! But nothing is impossible with You.*
>
> *In the meantime, Father, help me to direct my thoughts, energy and attitudes in a way that are pleasing to You O God. I love You and I thank You that Your timing and Your will are perfect. I am Your servant, Your child, Your beloved forever and ever... and so is he. We may be across oceans and time zones, but we are in the same Kingdom, so there is hope! Amen.*

I decided to confide in my two closest girlfriends, understanding full well the risk of looking like an absolute nutcase. However, as soon as they read the article, they understood where I was coming from. They too couldn't believe all the uncanny similarities.

We laughed about the strangeness of it all and agreed that the only thing to do really was to "give it to God." But what did it mean exactly to give this one over when this person seemed to flood my every thought? He even crept into my dreams. It became difficult to discern whether God was purposely making this man known to me, or whether this was a figment of my overly eager female imagination.

It didn't help to have Facebook, Google and YouTube—the ultimate stalking tools—tempting me to dig up more information on this person. It is possible in this technological age to find out about every detail of a person's life without even meeting them. But somehow God pulled me back; keeping me from giving my mind the green light to run wild with what "could be," envisioning every detail of our future life together. It wasn't that God didn't allow me to imagine and dream, but if I wanted to protect my heart from crossing into a land of false hopes and expectations, some boundaries had to be drawn.

Then God seemed to pull an odd reversal move on me. I had already drawn a line by deciding *not* to do any further research on Mr. Article Man. Then one day, I was looking up movie times on a Singapore website when I clicked on a movie trailer to see the preview of the movie. Out of the blue, a YouTube clip of this very person popped up on the screen—no joke. I did a double take to see if what I was actually seeing on the screen was real. I even tried retracing my steps to see if I could recreate what had just happened, but it didn't work. There was no logical way to explain it.

I must have looked like a stone-faced statue, sitting there at my desk. I was stunned, as if God had just zapped me with a taser gun. *Is this a sign or am I just going insane?* I wrote to God:

> *O Father, how in the heck did that just happen? Is there a reason why You showed me this? I can't help but think You are in on this. Thank you for how You are at work this moment... that this person is praying to You just as I am... that You will answer the desires of both our hearts... in Your perfect timing. Thank You for whatever Your will is...because I know it's good. Oh Lord, so much is uncertain, but one thing that IS for certain is YOU. I cling to that this moment. Amen.*

I took this "sighting" as an encouragement from the Lord to pray for this person, so that's what I started doing. From that day on, I prayed as a sister would for a brother: for his walk with God, his faith, his physical, mental and spiritual protection, provision, strength and success in his athletic career, for purity, wisdom, discernment, and vision for his life, for his desire to find a godly wife, for patience and hunger to know God more, for ears to hear and a heart to obey, and to feel and know and delight in our Father's love for him all the days of his life. Whether or not God would bring us together was outside my control. But choosing to stand in the gap for His children was never outside the will of the Father.

As I did this, more "signs" were coming from all different directions. For example, one woman I had met through the prison ministry I was involved in started sharing with me out of the blue one day how the Lord had divinely orchestrated her coming together with her husband while they were living on different continents. They corresponded for three months over the phone before meeting and were married shortly thereafter. She said to me, "Ali, nothing is impossible with God. He will orchestrate ANYTHING, even across oceans and continents, in order that His will comes to pass. Trust me, I know!" She shared this with me without even knowing about the article incident.

I also had several vivid dreams involving the person. Some involved meeting each other for the first time, while others involved our families and even locations of where were. I would wake up feeling like I had just been with him, it truly was crazy! I quit telling my friends about it and just kept writing them down as they came, and asking God to help me continue to live my life as usual.

It wasn't like I was searching for these signs. In fact, they would come at the most unexpected times, often making my heart jump with surprise. I knew God well enough to know that He would never try to purposely confuse me. In fact, according to John 16:13, He promises to guide us into all truth and tell us what is yet to come. It wasn't outside the realm of possibility that he was showing me things to come. All I could do was continue to put my trust in Him by pressing into His Word, as I waited for Him to bring clarity to the situation.

One morning, in the midst of asking the Lord for discernment on whether to believe the odd occurrences as signs of hope from Him or to brush them off as mere coincidences, I was led to Genesis 24. It's where Jacob's servant was sent on a mission to find Isaac's wife in a "faraway tribe." He asked the Lord for a specific "sign," that the right woman for Isaac would offer them a drink of water. Moments after the servant had asked God for a sign, Rebekah came to the well and "... quickly lowered the jar to her hands and gave him a drink" (Genesis 24:18). That was the exact "sign" that Jacob's servant had asked for from God. Without hesitation, he *knew* it was an answer to his specific request. The scripture then says Rebekah was taken back to marry Isaac, "...and he loved her" (Genesis 24:67).

The very same God that gave Jacob's servant a sign upon his request, was the very same God I served. But what gripped me about this story was the servant's unwavering faith. When he was given the specific sign he had asked for, he didn't sit there questioning whether it was from God or a figment of his imagination. He simply believed, because He knew God would answer. God was reminding me through this that just as He had answered the servant's earnest request, He had every intention to answer mine. I wrote out this prayer in my journal.

Lord, I am sorry for becoming impatient and doubting You. Please forgive me and continue to teach me how to wait patiently and in complete trust. Thank You for reminding me that You are working on all sides, in all things and at all times because You love me. Thank You that You want to answer my requests and that You will because I ask them in Jesus' precious name. Amen!

My adult mind demanded answers, solutions, reasons, clarifications and explanations, but I felt Him asking me to become like a child before Him. Just like Jacob's servant demonstrated the sweet simplicity of knowing God and believing, He wanted me to know that I know Him and simply believe. So I told Him out loud that I believed that the so-called signs that were coming onto my path were from Him.

As I continued to ask God for "signs" of encouragement that He wanted me to hold out hope for the man in the article, they kept coming. And with simple childlike obedience, I wrote every one of them down, whispering a silent, "Thank you Lord." How or when or where we would ever meet face-to-face was outside my control. All I could do was rest in my Father's arms, heeding the words of the psalmist who wrote, "Trust in Him at all times, O people; pour out your hearts to Him, for God is our refuge" (Psalm 62:8).

In the midst of all the uncertainty about my life and future, I felt closer than ever to my Father God. And that in itself was a "sign" from Heaven that everything was going according to His plan.

28

The Ministry of Marriage

Do nothing out of selfish ambition or vain conceit,
but in humility consider others better than yourselves.
Each of you should look not only to your own interests,
but also to the interests of others.

~ Philippians 2:3-4

All it took was one word for my marriage paradigm to shift like the plates of the earth in a 7.0 magnitude earthquake. The impact was profound, shattering the foundations upon which it was once held. The word was imbedded within an article a friend passed to me over email, "If you aspire to be a godly wife some day," it said, "what are you doing to prepare for that *ministry*?"[15]

Thinking of marriage as its own ministry invited a whole new wave of insight into the divine purposes God had for such a union. I looked up the very basic definition of ministry: "act of serving." Another Biblical source describes ministry as "a personal commission from God that labors toward the reconciliation of others to Christ through the gospel."[16] According to these two definitions, this meant my husband and I would be assigned to each other by God, to serve one another and labor in helping each other grow in our identity and calling in Christ. Wow. What a truly heavenly call.

This was so totally radical compared to the world's view how a marriage should be lived out. I was even convicted of my own consumer mentality, "What's in it for me?" or "How would this person meet *my* needs?" Thinking of marriage as a ministry brought me back to God's original and beautiful plan. It is about serving and ministering to one another in love—His love in us.

But just because two people were Christians, didn't mean all the pieces of a fruitful service-oriented marriage would magically just "fall into place." Quite the contrary, according to a recently married Christian couple, who were friends of mine. While they had completed all the marriage preparation classes and counseling sessions that were required under their church, they discovered the best preparation is really a matter of the heart—soberly reflecting, before God, on their own spiritual walk and maturity in Christ *before* deciding to marry. This would give God a chance to work on any "unfinished business" in their heart and character—like selfish habits and prideful attitudes— before entering marriage. "The more whole two people are before they enter into marriage," they said, "the more they can give to each other, rather than need from each other."

I wondered if I was whole enough in God to come together in a marriage. Was I in a position to effectively minister to the man I would call my husband? How was I supposed to prepare?

That answer came less than a week later as I walked into the room one ordinary Tuesday night where my fellowship meeting was usually held. I was shocked at what I saw. One of the leaders was on his knees, dipping a cloth into a water basin and scrubbing the feet of one the members of the worship team. I wondered for a moment if I was transported back to Biblical times. It was an extraordinary scene to say the least, but one that epitomized the life Jesus lived on earth—literally and metaphorically.

The talk that night was on serving others around us according to the "feet-washing" standard of Jesus. It was an incredible act of humility and the lowliest service someone could perform. But according to God's Word, we're given no choice in the matter. Jesus himself commanded it, "Now that I, your Lord and Teacher, have washed your feet, you also should wash one another's feet. I have set you an example that you should do as I have done for you" (John 13:14-15).

As we studied the very essence of servitude that night, through the example of Jesus washing the feet of His disciples, the Lord seemed to be saying, "And this, my dear Ali, is where the preparation for your spouse begins." Training myself to live with an "others-focused" mentality, rather than a "self-focused" one, would lay the groundwork for a godly marriage that thrived on hearts set on serving one another.

As this new revelation—of marriage as a ministry—sank into my spirit, I realized not only what a great privilege it was, but what a responsibility I had to continue to prepare for it. This would require living as a woman, not just hoping and praying to get married but as a woman intending to. This was different from obsessing over it or building it up to be something it wasn't. Rather, it was intentionally seeking to develop traits that would help me step into the shoes of a godly wife, aimed at serving my husband according to the feet-washing standards of Jesus.

Even though I didn't yet know whose wife I would be, I could still prepare for when I would meet him by seeking to become more whole in God—mind, body and soul. I began to imagine, with God's help, what kind of person would be the ultimate blessing to a husband. He led me to 1 Corinthians 13:4-8, where His definition of love is laid out. If I wanted to love my husband the way God intended, I would be a wife who:

- ♣ responded to my husband with patience and kindness
- ♣ was not envious, boastful, proud or rude towards him
- ♣ was not self-seeking or easily angered by him
- ♣ didn't keep a record of his wrongs
- ♣ refused to be deceitful, but always truthful with him
- ♣ protected his reputation, trusted him, always hoped for his good
- ♣ persevered through conflicts with him

Wow, I could see I had a long way to go before I would be able to love according to God's standard! But the point wasn't to strive to become the "perfect" wife on my own strength. It was realizing that it would only be through experiencing His love first in my life that would enable me to love someone in the fullness of the way He intended. In other words, our ministry of marriage would only be able to experience fruitful growth with Him at the center, working through us to serve one another.

I continued seeking God with a heart to become more whole and healthy in Him, trusting that it would prepare me for the time when I would say, "I do." Since I couldn't yet serve my husband in person, I could only serve him in prayer.

I pray for my husband this moment Lord. I pray you are putting a vision on his heart for both of us to be ministers of Your love to one another. I pray for divine protection over his thoughts, mind, heart, and body during this season. I pray that You are preparing him to meet me and become the godly husband You've destined Him to be. I pray for his health—

for any disease or sickness to leave his body in the name of Jesus.
I pray that His desires are in line with Yours and that he enjoys
spending time in You. Seeking You...worshiping You...delighting
in You...consulting You in all matters in his life. Thank You for
the beautiful and glorious plans you have for his and our life!
Thank You for Your appointed time, when You will call us to
serve together in Your ministry of marriage. Amen.

I became more serious than ever, not about finding the perfect mate, but about growing closer to God. This was the only way I could be sure that I would be fully equipped to minister to the man God called to be my husband. I couldn't wait for the day to come, when I would get to drop to my knees and wash his feet.

29

Soul Mates: A New Perspective

May the God of hope fill you with all joy and peace as you trust in him,
so that you may overflow with hope by the power of the Holy Spirit.

~ Romans 15:13

I met up with a friend one day to catch up after a fairly long absence from each other's lives. She had been married several months before, so our one-on-one time had dwindled drastically. They had finally settled into their new apartment, so I went over to check it out and to hang out like old times.

She had me rolling over in laughter as she gave me the scoop on what it was like to make the transition from "two to one." She detailed some of the more humorous little quirks and idiosyncrasies that drove her up the wall, like "He farts in his sleep" and "He has holes in his underwear but refuses to get new ones!"

The next thing I knew, tears were welling up in her eyes. *Her jokes were funny,* I thought, *but not that funny.* That's when the conversation did a complete 180 degree. What started out as lighthearted banter sharing about the initial road bumps in her marriage, turned into her confiding about some deeper problems they had going on, leading her to say this: "Ali, I was so certain he was my *soul mate*. But now I am not so sure."

Soul mate. I had heard this term thrown around so many times over the years, both in Christian and non-Christian circles—myself included. When I was a little girl, I even remember lying with my twin sister in bed late at night and we would dream about the day we would meet our "soul mates"—the one person in the whole entire world we were "destined" to marry. But when I listened to my friend that day, her heart troubled by the fact that she might have married the "wrong person," I felt compelled to get some answers on this one. I took the matter straight to God: "Lord, what's the deal with the whole "soul mate" thing—does it exist or not?"

What I discovered was that the term "soul mate" wasn't even a part of God's vast repertoire of vocabulary. However, separately, the word "soul" is mentioned hundreds of times in the Bible in various contexts. And God did say, "'It is not good for the man to be alone'" (Genesis 2:18), hence calling many of us to have "mates" in a marriage relationship. But nowhere in Scripture (that I was aware of) did God put the two together as "soul mate."

Did this mean that God couldn't lead two people together, according to His will? I liked to think that as I sought to be led by His wisdom in my daily circumstances with "…all *my* heart and with all *my* soul and with all *my* strength and with all *my* mind…" (Luke 10:27), then within this framework, God would lead me to one particular mate who was doing the same thing—loving Him with his whole heart and soul. Moreover, if I believed God meant what He said when He said He created us for "good works…prepared in advance for us to do..." (Ephesians 2:10), then it only made sense that God would do everything in His power to bring two people best suited to each other for accomplishing His Kingdom purposes as a unified couple. This was a sort of inner-monologue of reasoning with God I had going on in my head the days following meeting up with my distraught friend.

God then brought even more clarity to this "Ah-hah!" moment, through the life of a man named Bob. God was often generous like that. He would teach me something through His Word, and He would bring someone or some circumstance into the picture to illustrate and confirm His point. Such was the case with Bob, the Christian singer and songwriter who thought he was passing through Singapore as part of a worldwide tour to share his gift of music, but was really going to teach Ali on this topic of souls and mates—without even knowing it.

Bob spoke to our young adult's fellowship group that night. His wife Kathy couldn't make it, but we felt like she was there. As he shared his story, so much of it included her. He beamed as he told about their travels and adventures together, "My wife Kathy and I love seeking God together...Kath and I, we fall deeper in love with Jesus every day... Kath and I can attest, life gets sweeter as you grow older with God... Kath and I...Kath and I...Kath and I."

You'd think this was a newly-wedded couple still in their "honeymoon" phase. But here was a man who had been married for over twenty years, and yet he spoke of his relationship with Kathy with such a sweet reverence. As he gushed about her, God was glorified. Not only that, but joy was pouring out of him as he shared about their equal passion to serve, to know and to explore the endless depths of their Creator God together.

I was reminded of the superb movie *Chariots of Fire*, when Olympic gold medal winner and future missionary to China, Eric Liddell said, "When I run, I feel God's pleasure." When God gives us a gift, whether it be in the form of a talent or a person, and we live it out to the fullest, God is pleased. Just like the runner, Bob seemed to be saying, "When I am with my wife, I feel God's pleasure." It pleases God to bring together two people like Bob and Kathy, who love Him with "all their souls" and who wanted nothing more than to live out His kingdom purposes so that His true beauty and glory could shine through.

In the room-full of single people, I am sure I wasn't the only one thinking, "Wow, I hope to have that some day." It wasn't that their life was "perfect" and they experienced a problem-free life. Just like my newly-married friend, I am sure they had their share of problems and issues to work out. But the glue that seemed to hold them together was not some whimsical notion that they were "destined" to be together as soul mates, but their utter dependence on their God. He may have brought them together to be life-long "mates" while on this Earth, but it would require them to love God with all their hearts and "souls" in order for them to experience the fullness of joy and satisfaction He intended.

I imagined the day I would have a husband, when he would speak of me—his wife—and our life together the same way Bob did. He would say, "My wife Ali and I love worshiping God together...Ali and I, we really crave the presence of God...my wife Ali, she's the greatest blessing from God....Ali and I, we love to travel the world sharing and ministering God's Word...Ali and I..." I had never imagined in this way before. Actually hearing the words, "My wife Ali..." was strange, and yet it had a nice ring to it. It was as if God were saying to me, "Yes, Ali, you will one day be called someone's wife."

I looked forward to that day when God would answer the yearning of my heart—not for a soul mate but for a mate who loved God with all his soul. And who would say, "When I am with my wife Ali, I feel God's pleasure."

30

Finishing the Race

Perseverance must finish its work so that you may be
mature and complete, not lacking anything.

~ James 1:4

$\mathcal{T}$he day of the big race had finally arrived. This time it was
a marathon, a whopping 26-miler. Why I chose to run these grueling
races in the middle of the tropics, the Lord only knew. But I had
undergone months of disciplined training and could only hope I was
fully prepared. I sat at the kitchen table eating my oatmeal in the wee
hours of the morning in my Singapore apartment, literally praying for
divine strength. It was one of those times I decided to flip open the
Bible to a random page and well, it turned out not to be so random
after all, "...let us run with perseverance the race marked out for us...
fixing our eyes on Jesus, the author and perfecter of our faith... No
discipline seems pleasant at the time, but painful. Later on however, it
produces a harvest of righteousness and peace for those who have been
trained by it" (Hebrews 12:1-2, 11).

No joke—it really happened exactly in that way. I felt the Lord encouraging me that the training and discipline I had undergone to prepare for this race would pay off, and my "harvest of righteousness and peace" would be to finish the race strong. I showed up at the starting line with these verses written on my heart, determined and hopeful of finishing.

The fatigue started to kick in around mile 20. Just when I thought I might collapse into a flimsy, flattened pancake, I remembered to press into God, fixing my eyes on Him and trusting He would provide the strength, energy and morale I needed to continue until I reached the end. It was during this painful stretch of the race that I saw the parallel to the spiritual season God had me in. It was time to persevere, pressing on in my "race" of singleness, trusting He would help me finish strong.

I was in need of this kind of encouragement, due to a recent shift that had occurred in my heart. I had been feeling a new readiness to share my life with someone. To grow with someone. To be a blessing to someone. Though I had thoroughly embraced the season I was living in, my desire to build a future with someone had also increased in strength. Not seeing the end in sight, or knowing just how long it would be, wasn't always easy.

I liken it to the uncomfortable feeling just before a sneeze. The nose is bombarded by itches, tingles and tickles, but there's nothing you can do except wait for it to burst forth in a relieving shower of snot and saliva. Well, my heart was right there waiting for that sneeze, irritated by the tickles and anticipating the relief that was about to come—not in a shower of snot and saliva—but in the form of a relationship.

That day of the race, as my feet pitter-pattered through Singapore's squeaky clean streets—the cement damp from the hot and humid air—I heard the Lord's gentle but confirming whisper,

"Just keep moving forward champ. I promise to get you to the end." These words propelled me through each kilometer of the 26-mile race and gave me the encouragement I needed to press on through the season of singleness.

My legs had gone completely numb as I turned the final corner. Still, I found myself rejoicing with each step. As promised, He had brought me to the end, and rewarded—both physically and spiritually—for my perseverance. See, I realized that God didn't tell me to persevere just for the sake of it, but He says, "Perseverance must finish its work so that you may be mature and complete, not lacking anything" (James 1:4). I knew that as God had helped me finish the earthly race, He would help me finish the spiritual one *so that* I could be mature and complete in Him, lacking in nothing.

And just in case I needed more encouragement, God provided it at the church service I went to that very day of the race. Before the pastor began his sermon, he asked the congregation, "Has anyone ever run a marathon?" My friend Kelsey and I nudged each other and laughed—he had no idea that I had literally run a marathon a few hours before! Then he proceeded to preach on "running the spiritual race" and persevering until the end—just as the Lord had spoken to me earlier that morning. The sermon ended with the verse, "There is surely a future hope for you, and your expectation will not be cut off" (Proverbs 23:18).

I sat there and pondered my "expectation." I realized it wasn't for the actual blessings of God's promises themselves, but my expectation was in the One who promised. I had put my trust in Him, the God who was "...able to make all grace abound to you, so that in all things at all times, having all that you need, you will abound in every good work" (2 Chronicles 9:8). God had every area of my life covered. And He expected nothing less than for me to expect in His sufficiency in all things. I wrote this prayer in my journal as I waited in expectation for that "sneeze" to come.

> *Lord, you know all my hopes and desires because You put them there. My expectation is in You because I take You at Your word when You promise to provide for my every need. Thank you Lord that my perseverance is finishing its work so that I will be mature and complete, as I prepare to share my life with someone whom You have chosen for me. I leave the details to You O God, as I seek Your face. And I wait with joyful expectation now and until the end of this season's race. I love you. Amen.*

I now had a new determination to persevere through the season—joyfully and with expectation. Though I still had some distance to run in this season's race, He was asking me to trust that the end was near. Some aches, pains and moments of fatigue would come along the way, but just as the training and discipline I underwent to prepare for the marathon paid off in the end, I trusted that the spiritual and character "training" I was undergoing to prepare for a marriage relationship would pay off too.

I wasn't sure how the details of my future would play out. But I could be absolutely sure of one thing: that He would provide everything I needed, at exactly the right time, every step of the way. It was up to Him whether it would include putting someone else in the race who would come run alongside me, and who would take my hand to cross the finish line together, marking a triumphant end to one season and a beautiful start to the next.

In the meantime, all I could do was keep running forward, with my eyes fixed on Jesus.

Conclusion

His Beautiful Bride

I debated whether or not to even write a conclusion. What did I have to conclude? The fact is, I'm still single. Still waiting on God. Still trusting that the key to my heart is safe in His hands. It's not like I'm a bride with a groom by my side. *That* would have made a great conclusion.

But then God reminded me of something. I am a bride—His bride. The night I surrendered my heart to Him and let Jesus become not just my Savior, but Lord over *every* area of my life, was the night He became my eternal husband. His constant company and companionship have brought me under His direction, wisdom and guidance, making me more whole in Him. Now it's up to Him, whether He will steer me into a marriage relationship to become an earthly bride.

While He takes care of the details regarding the desires of my heart, my job is simple: to continue seeking first His Kingdom in all things—hearing and obeying what He is telling me to do— and trusting that His words are true, that "He has made everything beautiful in its time."

THE END. Of the book, that is.

My love journey continues...

until someone is given the key... who will it be?

You might just have to read the next book to find out.

My Prayer for You:

I pray, beloved reader—that you and your own love story are being made beautiful according to His perfect timing. Whatever your age, stage or relationship status, He has you right where you are, just the way you are. He's waiting for you to accept the invitation to your very own marriage supper, not just as a guest but as His beautiful bride. Will you say "I do?"

If I may, I would like to say a prayer for you:

Dear Lord, I pray for my beautiful sister reading these words right now. Meet her right where she is at. Speak directly to her heart. Show her that you are real and that you have a specific and special plan for her life. Father, I ask that you stir in her a desire to know you more and you teach her how to do this. Show her how to have a deep and meaningful, living and vibrant relationship with you. Open her ears to hear your voice and give her a willingness to obey. I ask Lord, that whatever her past relationship history is, that you heal any old hurts or wounds and that you restore her heart back to its complete, whole and healthy state that you designed it to be in Jesus' name. And that if is your will for her to enter into a marriage relationship that you start preparing her right now for that ministry. Lord, thank you now for every desire in her heart and that you will answer every single one. Please be with her as she waits patiently for your plans to be unveiled. Fill her with all peace and joy as she trusts in you, so she may be filled with hope by the power of your Holy Spirit (Romans 15:13). Protect her and provide for each and every one of her needs. May she rest in the safety of your arms and may she feel your loving embrace. Comfort, console and continue to mold her into the likeness of your son, as she so bravely and boldly entrusts the key to her precious heart into your hands. Amen!

If you would like to entrust the key to your very own into God's hands—as a symbolic act of you putting your full trust in Him—then say this prayer:

Dear Lord, this moment I would like to give you the key to my heart to have and to hold, to protect and to mold, according to Your will, not mine. Remove my fears Lord and help me to let you take the lead when it comes to matters of my heart, trusting that You know what's best for my life. Take me on a journey with You to learn to hear Your voice and obey You in all things so that I may become more whole in You. Thank you that You are faithful and You will do it. In Jesus name I pray, Amen!

Verses to Write on Your Heart

Dear Reader,

I want to share the following verses that made a significant impact on my journey and continue to do so. God has used these very words—His Words—to speak directly to my heart. Whether they brought comfort, consolation, instruction, or guidance, they have helped me to have a greater understanding of who God is and who He has called me to be. I pray they may speak to you in their own unique way, helping to draw you closer to His heart and purpose for your life. May you experience the fullness of His love, grace, joy and strength wherever you are. Be blessed sister!

Contentment/Joy

Psalm 92:4-5

For you make me glad by your deeds, O LORD;
I sing for joy at the works of your hands.
How great are your works, O LORD,
how profound your thoughts!

Romans 11:33

Oh, the depth of the riches of the wisdom
and knowledge of God!

Isaiah 55:12

You will go out in joy and be led forth in peace;
the mountains and hills will burst into song before you,
and all the trees of the field will clap their hands.

Psalm 23:1-2

The LORD is my shepherd, I shall not want.
He makes me lie down in green pastures;
He leads me beside quiet waters.
He restores my soul;
He guides me in the paths of righteousness
For His name's sake.

John 7:38

Whoever believes in me, as the Scripture has said,
streams of living water will flow from within him.

Micah 6:8

He has showed you, O man, what is good.
And what does the LORD require of you?
To act justly and to love mercy and
to walk humbly with your God.

Philippians 4:4

Rejoice in the Lord always, I say it again, rejoice!

Nehemiah 8:10

The Joy of the Lord is your strength.

Endurance

James 1:2-4

Consider it pure joy, my brothers, whenever you face trials of
many kinds, because you know that the testing of your faith
develops perseverance. Perseverance must finish its work so that
you may be mature and complete, not lacking anything.

Galatians 6:9
Let us not become weary in doing good,
for at the proper time we will reap a harvest
if we do not give up.

Philippians 3:13
Brothers, I do not consider myself yet to have taken hold of it.
But one thing I do: Forgetting what is behind and straining toward
what is ahead, I press on toward the goal to win the prize
for which God has called me heavenward in Christ Jesus.

2 Timothy 1:7
God did not give us a spirit of timidity, but a spirit of power,
of love and of self-discipline

Hebrews 10:23-24
...Let us draw near to God with a sincere heart
in full assurance of faith, having our hearts sprinkled to
cleanse us from a guilty conscience and
having our bodies washed with pure water.
Let us hold unswervingly to the hope we profess,
for he who promised is faithful.

Friendship

Proverbs 13:20
He who walks with the wise grows wise,
but a companion of fools suffers harm.

John 15:15

I no longer call you servants, because a servant does not know
his master's business. Instead, I have called you friends,
for everything that I learned from my Father
I have made known to you.

Romans 12:15

Rejoice with those who rejoice;
mourn with those who mourn.

Hebrews 10:24-25

And let us consider how we may spur one another on toward
love and good deeds. Let us not give up meeting together,
as some are in the habit of doing, but let us encourage one another—
and all the more as you see the Day approaching.

Hope

Jeremiah 29:11

"For I know the plans I have for you," declares the LORD,
"plans to prosper you and not to harm you,
plans to give you hope and a future."

Romans 15:13

May the God of hope fill you with all joy and peace
as you trust in him, so that you may overflow with hope
by the power of the Holy Spirit.

Psalm 25:4-5

Show me your ways, O LORD, teach me your paths;
guide me in your truth and teach me for you are God my Savior,
and my hope is in you all day long.

Psalm 119:147

I rise before dawn and cry for help;
I have put my hope in your word.

Isaiah 40:31

Those who hope in the LORD will renew their strength.
They will soar on wings like eagles;
they will run and not grow weary, they will walk and not be faint

Micah 7:7

But as for me, I watch in hope for the LORD,
I wait for God my Savior; my God will hear me.

Loneliness

Psalm 41:11-12

I know that you are pleased with me for my enemy does not
triumph over me. In my integrity you uphold me and
set me in your presence forever.

John 11:41

Then Jesus looked up and said,
"Father, I thank you that you have heard me.
I knew that you always hear me..."

Genesis 28:15

I am with you and will watch over you wherever you go,
and I will bring you back to this land.
I will not leave you until
I have done what I have promised you.

Joshua 1:9

Be strong and courageous. Do not be terrified;
do not be discouraged, for the LORD your God
will be with you wherever you go.

Isaiah 41:13

For I am the Lord your God,
who takes hold of your right hand and says to you,
'Do not fear, I will help you.'

Psalm 38:9

All my longings lie open before you, O Lord;
my sighing is not hidden from you.

Obedience

John 14:21

Whoever has my commands and obeys them,
he is the one who loves me.
He who loves me will be loved by my Father,
and I too will love him and show myself to him.

John 10:27

My sheep listen to my voice;
I know them, and they follow me.

1 John 3:24

Those who obey his commands live in him, and he in them.
And this is how we know that he lives in us:
We know it by the Spirit he gave us.

Psalm 25:9-10

He guides the humble in what is right and teaches them his way.
All the ways of the LORD are loving and
faithful for those who keep the demands of his covenant.

Deuteronomy 30:9-10

The LORD will again delight in you and make you prosperous,
just as he delighted in your fathers, if you obey the LORD your God
and keep his commands and decrees that are written in this
Book of the Law and turn to the LORD your God
with all your heart and with all your soul.

Deuteronomy 30:14

The word is very near you; it is in your mouth and
in your heart so you may obey it.

Joshua 1:8

Do not let this Book of the Law depart from your mouth;
meditate on it day and night, so that you may be careful to do
everything written in it. Then you will be prosperous and successful.

Proverbs 1:33

Whoever listens to me will live in safety and will be at ease,
without fear of harm.

Proverbs 8:10-11

Choose my instruction instead of silver, knowledge rather than
choice gold, for wisdom is more precious than rubies,
and nothing you desire can compare with her.

Security/Worth/Beauty

1 Peter 3:3

Your beauty should not come through outward adornment...instead it
should be that of your inner self, the unfading beauty of a gentle and
quiet spirit, which is of great worth in God's sight.

Proverbs 12:4

A wife of noble character is her husband's crown,
but a disgraceful wife is like decay in his bones.

Isaiah 61:10

I delight greatly in the LORD; my soul rejoices in my God.
For he has clothed me with garments of salvation and arrayed me in
a robe of righteousness, as a bridegroom adorns his head like a priest,
and as a bride adorns herself with her jewels.

Colossians 3:12

As God's chosen people, holy and dearly loved,
clothe yourselves with compassion, kindness, humility,
gentleness and patience.

Psalm 90:17

May the beauty of the Lord our God rest upon us;
establish the work of our hands for us—yes,
establish the work of our hands.

1 Corinthians 3:16-17
Don't you know that you yourselves are God's temple and that
God's Spirit lives in you? If anyone destroys God's temple,
God will destroy him; for God's temple is sacred,
and you are that temple.

1 Corinthians 6:19-20
Do you not know that your body is a temple of the Holy Spirit,
who is in you, whom you have received from God?
You are not your own; you were bought at a price.
Therefore honor God with your body.

Ephesians 2:10
For we are God's workmanship,
created in Christ Jesus to do good works,
which God prepared in advance for us to do.

Isaiah 43:1
I have summoned you by name, you are mine.

Psalm 45:11
The king is enthralled by your beauty.
Honor Him for He is your Lord.

Seeking

Hebrews 11:6
And without faith it is impossible to please God,
because anyone who comes to him must believe that he exists and
that he rewards those who earnestly seek him.

Matthew 6:33

But seek first his kingdom and his righteousness,
and all these things will be given to you as well.

John 15:7

If you remain in me and my words remain in you,
ask whatever you wish, and it will be given you.

Psalm 42:1

As the deer pants for streams of water,
so my soul pants for you, O God. My soul thirsts for God,
for the living God.

Matthew 7:7

Ask, and it will be given to you; seek, and you will find; knock,
and it will be opened to you.

Isaiah 55:6

Seek the LORD while he may be found;
call on him while he is near.

Psalm 37:4

Delight yourself in the Lord and
He will give you the desires of your heart.

Trust/Surrender

Psalm 62:8

Commit your way to the LORD,
Trust also in Him, and He will do it.

Psalm 143:8
Cause me to hear your loving-kindness in the morning, for on you do I lean and in you do I trust. Cause me to know the way where in I should walk, for I lift up my inner self to you. (AMP)

Philippians 4:4-7
The Lord is near. Do not be anxious about anything, but in everything, by prayer and petition, with thanksgiving, present your requests to God. And the peace of God, which transcends all understanding, will guard your hearts and your minds in Christ Jesus.

1 Corinthians 2:9
No eye has seen, no ear has heard, no mind has conceived what God has prepared for those who love him.

Jeremiah 33:3
Call to me and I will answer you and tell you great and unsearchable things you do not know.

Jeremiah 17:7
But blessed is the man who trusts in the LORD, whose confidence is in him.

Philippians 4:19
God will meet all your needs according to His glorious riches in Christ Jesus.

Psalm 86:11
Teach me your way, O LORD, and I will walk in your truth; give me an undivided heart, that I may fear your name.

Luke 10:27

Love the Lord your God with all your heart and with all your soul
and with all your strength and with all your mind...

Isaiah 12:2-3

I will trust and not be afraid. The LORD, the LORD,
is my strength and my song; he has become my salvation."
With joy you will draw water from the wells of salvation.

Waiting

Psalm 27:14

Wait on the Lord; be of good courage,
and he should strengthen your heart.

Lamentations 3:24

I say to myself, "The LORD is my portion;
therefore I will wait for him."

Isaiah 64:4

For from days of old they have not heard or perceived by ear,
nor has the eye seen a God besides You,
Who acts in behalf of the one who waits for Him.

Ecclesiastes 3:1

There is a time for everything, and a season for
every activity under heaven.

Psalm 37:7

Be still before the LORD and wait patiently for him;
do not fret when men succeed in their ways,
when they carry out their wicked schemes.

Psalm 33:20

Our soul waits for the LORD;
He is our help and our shield.

Wisdom

Proverbs 8:10-12

Choose my instruction, instead of silver, knowledge rather than
choice gold, for wisdom is more precious than choice rubies,
and nothing you desire can compare with her.

Proverbs 8:33

Listen to my instruction and be wise; do not ignore it.

Proverbs 13:18

He who ignores discipline comes to poverty and shame,
but whoever heeds correction is honored.

James 1:5

If any of you lacks wisdom, he should ask God, who gives generously
to all without finding fault, and it will be given to him.

1 Corinthians 1:30
It is because of him that you are in Christ Jesus,
who has become for us wisdom from God—that is,
our righteousness, holiness and redemption.

Proverbs 15:22
Plans fail for lack of counsel,
but with many advisors they succeed.

Reflection & Discussion Guide

Unlocking Treasures of Truth

Chapter 1 - The Canvas of My Past

1. In what ways did the relationships you grew up around shape your beliefs and attitudes about love, relationships and marriage? What kind of impact has it had in your own life? Anything you'd like to change?

2. Prayerfully review any past romantic relationships and ask God to reveal through His Holy Spirit what you can learn. If you haven't had a romantic relationship, ask God if you are ready to have one and to help you wait on His timing.

3. Do you think it's important to be with someone who shares your faith? Why or why not?

Chapter 2 - Taking God Out of the Suitcase

1. Prayerfully ponder what role your faith plays in your life.

2. Is your faith just another garment in your suitcase or do you wear it 24/7? Have you let God into your entire life? If not, what's holding you back?

3. Is your life an accurate representation of your belief system? What are some ways people might notice your faith without you even saying it?

Chapter 3 - Serving My Heart on a Silver Platter

1. Have you ever been in a situation when you "served your heart on a silver platter" to someone too soon? What happened and what can you learn from it?

2. Prayerfully ponder your longing or desire to be with another person. Are you letting this desire control your mood, behavior and thought life? How can you practice directing your desires to God?

3. What are your thoughts on dating? Do you see any value in the Filipino way of courtship?

Chapter 4 - Accepting Closed Doors

1. When was a time you experienced a direct answer to prayer? How did you know? Talk it over with a friend.

2. Has God ever closed a door on a prayer you prayed? How did you respond?

3. How often do you go to God before making a decision involving your heart? What are some ways you can learn to be led by Him in this area?

Chapter 5 - Giving My Own Green Light

1. Are there times when you give your own green light and drag God along for the ride? Prayerfully ask God to reveal these times to you.

2. Have you ever experienced a broken heart? How did you get there? Have you healed from it? Ask God what needs to be restored and how to avoid it happening again.

3. Are you willing to wait for His green light when it comes to relationships? Ask Him for a greater desire to want to follow Him.

Chapter 6 - The "List"

1. Are you conscious of the desires dwelling inside your heart? Have you brought them before God?

2. How specifically are you talking to God? Talk this over with a friend.

3. How do you feel about the whole list thing? Have you made a list? If so, what's on it? If not, what's holding you back?

Chapter 7- The Center of His Palm

1. Are there any fears that are preventing you from experiencing God's love and hearing God's voice in your life?

2. God does not move on account of geography, but of proximity to Him— what does this mean to you?

3. Prayerfully evaluate where you are. Are you in the center of His palm? Are there any active steps you could take to get there?

Chapter 8 - "Just Friends"

1. How many female versus male friends do you have? Do you find yourself relating more to women or men? Ask God to reveal any imbalances or behaviors that are not pleasing to Him.

2. Have you ever experienced a time when you felt your heart getting attached to someone with whom you were "just friends?" What was it that caused the boundaries to get blurred?

3. Do you think it's possible for two marriage-minded people to be just friends? Do you think there are risks involved? If so, what are they?

Chapter 9 - Positioning to Receive

1. When was a time that you heard God speak directly to your situation? What did He say and how did you respond?

2. Proverbs 4:23 says, "Above all else, guard your heart, for it is the wellspring of life." What does this verse mean to you? What are some practical ways you can guard your heart?

3. How are you spending your time and with whom? If you are trusting God to provide a spouse, are you in a position to receive from Him?

Chapter 10 - Thank God for Godly Counsel

1. Examine your motives for obeying God. Is it out of obligation or your love for Him?

2. Do you go to God to seek instruction before making a decision? How can you incorporate your faith into your decision-making?

3. Do you have someone you can go to for godly counsel? Pick a person in your community and decide to share your life with them. Ask them if they would be willing to pray with you and advise you regarding the desires of your heart.

Chapter 11 - Point of Surrender

1. The author is pointing to a difference between opening your heart to God and surrendering it. What do you think?

2. On a scale of one to ten (one being the least), how much do you trust God with the desires of your heart?

3. Have you entrusted the key of your heart to God? If not, what's holding you back? Ask God to remove any hindrance or fear so that you can trust Him in all things.

Chapter 12 - Blessings of Obedience

1. The author says that God gave her the freedom to choose His ways. What does this mean to you? Recall a time when you were given a choice to obey.

2. Meditate on the fruits of the Spirit found in Galatians 5. Which areas of your life are you experiencing His "fruits" and which areas are lacking?

3. Do you find it difficult to follow God when you don't understand why? Look up Isaiah 55:9. Ask God to help you surrender the need to fully understand His ways.

Chapter 13 - Waiting in Action

1. The author says one way the Lord speaks to her is through repetition. Have you ever experienced this? In what other ways does God make His voice known to you?

2. What are you waiting on God for in this season? Do you feel discouraged more than you feel hopeful? The author suggests finding encouragement in God's Word. Find some verses that bring you hope and write them down or memorize them.

3. Do your thoughts, attitudes and words reflect your full trust in God? Instead of dwelling on the negative, what are some positive ways you can embrace the process of waiting? Ask God for wisdom in showing you how to spend your time.

Chapter 14 - A Game of Seek-and-Find

1. Does a game of hide-and-seek or seek-and-find describe your relationship with God?

2. Are you seeking first His kingdom and His righteousness in all things (Matthew 6:33)? The author suggests spending more time with God. What are some ways you can cultivate a lifestyle of seeking Him?

3. Rate your passion for God on a scale of one to ten (one being the least). Discuss with a friend. Ask God to give you a greater hunger to know Him and seek after Him in all things.

Chapter 15 - Holy Guacamole

1. Ask God to help you distinguish between fantasy and reality as you imagine and pray for your future life partner.

2. Does your life reflect the kind of quality and standard you are praying for in a mate? Prayerfully ask God to shift your focus from the kind of life partner you want to becoming the woman He wants you to be.

3. If God were to bring along your life partner right now, would He see a godly woman? Is your inner beauty outshining your outer adornment? Ask God to show you how you can increase your inner beauty.

Chapter 16 - Be Content, Not Confined

1. Are there people around you "graduating" to the next phase in life? How does it make you feel? How can you practice celebrating with them and trusting God has His own timing for you?

2. Are you ever tempted to think your life will "start" once you are married? Ask God to expose any mindsets that are not of Him. What is He calling you to do now in the season you are in?

3. Do you feel content with what you have or confined by what you don't have? Tell a friend. Pray that God will give you eyes to see all He has placed before you in this season and to give you His joy as your strength (Nehemiah 8:10).

Chapter 17 - Skype Dates with God

1. The author speaks of God's longing to connect with His children. Do you long to connect with Him as much as your human friends and loved ones? Ask Him to increase your desire to strengthen your relationship with Him.

2. The author highlights the verse, "Be still and know that I am God" (Psalm 46:10), as well as Martin Luther's words, "Be still and let Him mold you." Have you experienced "being still" before God? Why is it an important part of the Christian life?

3. Have you picked a special meeting place for you and God? If not, pick one and set a regular meeting time with God each day. Practice pouring your heart out to Him and listening to His voice.

Chapter 18 - Refusing the Pressure Cooker

1. What are the pressures surrounding marriage in your culture? Are you giving in to the "pressure cooker" paradigm? How can you defend from inquisitive "arrows" flying your way?

2. The author says, "God helped me to see marriage not as a completion of my life and happiness, but as a complement to who I was in Christ." What is your current view of marriage? Ask God to give you a perspective in line with His will.

3. If you truly believe God's timing is perfect and He remains faithful to His promise laid out in the Bible, what is there to worry about? Do you find yourself struggling to fend off worry, fear and doubt about your future? Pick out some of your favorite promises in God's Word. Ask Him to help you believe them to a point that it removes all your worries.

Chapter 19 - Awed by His Awesomeness

1. Have you ever been confronted with a realization similar to the author's that your level of trust in God was "shaped like a small box" that you had put God, and all He is capable of doing, into? Ask God to help bring you to a higher level of trust. For example, is there anything He might be asking you to do but you're not doing because you think it's impossible?

2. Meditate on Proverbs 1:7, "The fear of the Lord is the beginning of wisdom." What is your current understanding of "fearing" God? In what ways might fear of God lead to making wise choices?

3. Practice meditating on God with a new sense of awe and reverence. Ask Him to show you a new vision of "His majesty, His greatness, His holiness, His perfect righteousness, His irresistible power, and His sovereign grace." Keep a journal close by and see how magnifying God's greatness might change your perspective on your future or a current situation you are facing.

Chapter 20 - A Good Laugh

1. When a "person of interest" comes into your path, how do you talk to God about it?

2. Prayerfully consider what you are waiting on God for—A promotion? A spouse? For your family to know God? Are there ever times you want to manipulate the process to speed things up? How can you practice waiting patiently on God's timing?

3. The author points out that God wants us to come to Him not only for serious matters, but for light-hearted ones too. Prayerfully evaluate your level of joy in the Lord. Meditate on Nehemiah 8:10, "*The Joy of the Lord is your strength*" and ask God how this can become a reality in your life.

Chapter 21 - Staying on the Potter's Wheel

1. If you have siblings, how have each of your love journeys played out? Pray for whatever season they are in and ask God's help to enjoy whatever season He has you in.

2. Do you ever find yourself comparing with other people, perhaps in relation to what they have and what you don't have? Ask God to help you trust in the reasons for the seasons He has brought you through.

3. If God is the potter and you are His clay, what might be some "rough edges" He might want to smooth out during this season? Ask Him to reveal these things to you and for help to remove them.

Chapter 22 - Not Every Man You Meet is a Potential Mate

1. Recall a time when you became aware of those familiar "butterflies" the author speaks of. Ask God to help you strike a balance between allowing yourself to feel and exercising self-control.

2. What does "guard your heart" mean to you? Why does the Bible instruct us in such a way? How can you practice letting God guard your heart?

3. Prayerfully evaluate your mindset. Do you have a one-track mind when it comes to meeting people of the opposite sex? Practice seeing each person you meet as a child of God first, and let God lead you from there.

Chapter 23 - Serendipity

1. Can you relate to the author's question, "*Lord, did I mess up your plan?*" How does your perspective change when you reflect upon the verse from Jeremiah 1:5, "Before I formed you in the womb, I knew you"?

2. What are your thoughts on serendipity or moments when good things seem to "fall into place?" Do things like good luck, chance and fate play into God's vocabulary?

3. The author points to the verse in Deuteronomy 30:9, "The Lord will again delight in you." Imagine the Lord taking great delight in you, this moment, wherever you are. What are some ways you can delight in Him?

Chapter 24 - Lonely but Not Alone

1. Imagine God lifting you onto His lap and saying, "My child, tell me what is troubling your heart." Write a letter to God telling Him every longing and yearning of your heart.

2. Have you experienced loneliness on your road of waiting? Make a list of your favorite verses from the Book of Psalms and practice giving voice to these yearnings in your heart.

3. Reflect on the idea of thanksgiving as an expression of an emotion versus and act of will. Make a list of all the things you are thankful for during the season you are in, regardless of how you feel.

Chapter 25 - Total Life-Sharing Intimacy

1. Would you define your life-style as independent or interdependent? Ask God where you can make adjustments that will align your life to His intended purposes.

2. When you think of "intimacy" what comes to mind? The Bible says, "if we walk in the light, God himself being the light, we also experience a *shared life* with one another" (1 John 1:7, MSG). Why does walking with God mean we also must walk closely with others? Discuss with a friend.

3. The author speaks of the importance of having at least one or two "soul-level" friends to build each other up in our godly identity, to pray with and encourage, and to expose areas that are not functioning properly. Do you have any soul-level friends? If so, reflect on how they have added value along your road of waiting. If not, pray and ask God to bring you a soul-level friend with whom you can share your life totally.

Chapter 26 - A Lesson on Yokes

1. What do you make of Paul's instruction to the Corinthian church, "Do not be yoked together with unbelievers" (2 Corinthians 6:14)? Discuss this passage in light of David Lipscomb's comment, "To be unequally yoked would be to be...persons that do not harmonize in purpose, walk, and life." Discuss with a friend what you think it means to be "equally yoked" in marriage.

2. Whenever you meet someone new, what kind of "big picture" questions should you ask yourself?

3. Has God given you vision and calling for your life? How does this fit in with God's divine plan for marriage with the man as the head of the household? Ask God for wisdom and discernment in knowing how to blend with a mate. If not, ask God to prepare you to play a supporting role in the calling of your partner.

Chapter 27 - Signs or Insanity?

1. Read Genesis 24. Have you ever asked God to give you a "sign" as Jacob's servant did? Did God answer? Practice praying specifically and expecting Him to answer.

2. The author cites John 16:13, "The Spirit of the Lord will guide you into all truth and tell you what is yet to come." What does this verse mean to you? Has the Lord ever told you things to come before they happened? Take this promise to God, asking the Holy Spirit to give you prophetic insight into your own future.

3. The author talks about drawing lines so as not to cross into a "fantasy-land of false hopes and expectations." Do you find it hard to control your thought and imagination when it comes to your future hopes and dreams? What are some practical boundaries you can set like limiting time on the Internet, Facebook, TV and reading gossip magazines to protect your heart and mind from "running wild" with possibilities that may not be from God? Pick a friend to hold you accountable to your boundaries and journal any differences you feel as a result.

Chapter 28 - The Ministry of Marriage

1. What is your current view of the *purpose of marriage*? How is it similar or different to God's view of marriage as a ministry?

2. The author points to Jesus washing the feet of His disciples (John 13:5) as an example of the kind of humility God desires us demonstrate in our human relationships, including marriage. How can you apply this "feet-washing" standard of humility to your life right now? In what ways can you serve those God has put in your path during this season?

3. Meditate on God's definition of love found in 1 Corinthians 13:4-8. Envision living out this standard of love within a marriage some day. Ask God to reveal the character traits and shortcomings you can work on *now* that will move you towards becoming the wife who will be a blessing to her husband.

Chapter 29 - Soul Mates: A New Perspective

1. What is your notion of "soul mates?" In what context have you used the term or heard it used? Do you think it supports God's perspective? Why or why not?

2. The author mentions the movie, *Chariots of Fire* when Olympic gold medal winner and future missionary to China, Eric Liddell said, "When I run, I feel God's pleasure." What do you think he meant? Ask yourself, "Is God pleased with the way I am living out my talents and relationships?" If not, ask God what you need to change so that you can experience pleasure through His being pleased.

3. The author imagines hearing the words, "My wife Ali and I...." If you are not married yet, try inserting your name. What would your husband say about you and your relationship? What are some things that you desire to be a part of your future marriage so that God is glorified through it?

Chapter 30 - Finishing the Race

1. Have you ever run a race? Meditate on the perseverance verses in Hebrews 12:1-2, 11. What areas in your life are calling for perseverance?

2. The author cites Proverbs 23:18, "There is surely a future hope for you, and your expectation will not be cut off." Evaluate your expectations. Are they in line with God's promises? Ask God to give you a heart of expectancy for the things He promises.

3. Prayerfully reflect on what 2 Corinthians 9:8 is saying, that "God is able to make all grace abound to you, so that in all things at all times, having all that you need, you will abound in every good work." Do you believe God can provide for your every need? Talk to Him about your needs and ask Him to show you.

Notes

1. "The More I Seek You,": ©1999 Zach Neese / Gateway Create Publishing / Integrity's Praise Music (all admin. by Integrity Praise) BMI-CCLLI#444791

2. "A Girl's Guide to Marrying Well," found at www.boundless.org/girls

3. "Jesuswalk" website, Dr. Ralph Wilson

4. "A Homily of Waiting", by Henri Nouwen

5. Hebrews 11:1

6. Carol Cooper, "Living Life by the Spirit: Prayer in a New Dimension" Seminar

7. Psalm 23:2-3

8. Psalm 16:11

9. "Sanctuary": © 1982 Whole Armor Publishing / Full Armor Music, words and music by John W. Thompson and Randy Scruggs

10. Jeremiah 29:11

11. Hebrews 5:7

12. http://www.brainyquote.com/words/in/independence177752.html

13. David Lipscomb's commentary on Paul's Second Epistle, pg 93

14. "Unequally Yoked Together: Does 2 Corinthians 6:14 Apply to Marriage?" by Al Maxey, found on http://www.gracecentered.com/unequally_yoked.htm

15. "A Girl's Guide to Marrying Well," found at www.boundless.org/girls

16. Collide Magazine, "A Biblical Definition of Ministry in a Technological Age," by Stephen Presley

Acknowledgments

$\mathscr{I}$was honestly in complete and utter amazement when I first saw the finished product of this book—not at what I was able to do, but what God was able to do through me. From the very beginning my prayer was, "Okay God, this is Your book... now do what You will!" What I discovered is that it really is possible to "do all things through Him who strengthens me" (Philippians 4:13, NASB). It is only by His divine power, grace and strength that this project was brought to completion. So, thank you my Lord. What a privilege it is to serve You through writing.

I would like to extend my deepest gratitude to the many "angels" sent to help me along in this process.

Thank you...

+ ***Mom*** - for your unconditional love, prayers and support and for acting as my "sound board" whenever I needed a listening ear. Your unwavering enthusiasm for life has had a profound impact on my faith journey and I am grateful.

+ ***Dad, Jenny, Courtney, Kelli, Aaron and Abe*** - your constant prayers and encouragement meant the world to me, even by just asking "How's the book coming along?"

- ✦ *Campus Crusade Mass Media Team* - for your unwavering commitment, enthusiasm and hard work in pushing this book out at the speed of light! Especially Hui Lin, what a joy to work with such a "kindred spirit," equally passionate about reaching singles around the globe!

- ✦ *Ken* - for your creative genius and direction for the cover design. What a blessing it was to work together for His Kingdom purposes! Your heart to serve others is truly an inspiration. Jade - for offering your wise opinions regarding the book at timely moments and for your constant love throughout the process.

- ✦ *Ruth Soh* - for your kind and gentle nature behind the camera. You are so talented and I am so filled with gratitude for the work that you did.

- ✦ *Norhaya* - for your willingness to be a connector. Your presence brought warmth and calm to the process at the time when it was most needed.

- ✦ *Carolina Ong* - for your expertise in reading the final manuscript.

- ✦ *Susan* - for your prompt responses to my millions of questions and your willingness to share the wealth of knowledge and wisdom you've gained from having gone through this process yourself. You were such a blessing, really.

- ✦ *Kathy Tyers* - for your "laser eyes!" I couldn't have asked for a better editor - fast, efficient, honest and encouraging. You helped bring my writing to the next level.

- ✦ *Akiko* - for your willingness to read my manuscript all the way through! It was your initial positive feedback that gave me confidence heading into the editing phase.

+ *Kate* - How good is God that we were both writing at the same time - in Singapore! Your warmth, hugs and cups of joe during those long hours of working on the manuscript were invaluable. I couldn't have finished without the love God poured through you!

+ *Kelsey* - How gracious God is to have placed us in the exact same season at the exact same time living under the exact same roof. Your timely prayers, words of encouragement and listening ears were like treasures sent straight from heaven. Our babies are out!

+ *Jiamin* - for being the best writing buddy in the world! What a joy to get to journey alongside each other. Your prayers, feedback and encouragement in the early phases were priceless. We made it!

+ *Readers - Sherlee, Gracie, Grace, Kelsey, Kate, Katie, Carol, Cathy, Lillie, Claire, Sue-Ann, Janette, Jacqueline, Val, Marie, Hannah* - for your willingness to read the chapters I sent you. The feedback you gave was so helpful in improving my manuscript. What a blessing it is to get to share this journey with you - my cherished sisters!

+ *All the women who shared their stories with me*, which added value and depth to the themes in this book. And a special thanks to those who graciously sent endorsements, feedback and advice to spur me along in this exhilarating adventure.

+ *Marcus* - for your advise in legal matters. Jeanne - for always willing to give a listening ear. Your love and prayers meant a lot along the roller coaster ride of this process.

+ *Pastor John and Nancy* - for providing a place of refuge and restoration each week at church. Your teachings, prayers and timely "check-in" chats kept me fueled and nourished in the writing process.

+ **Paul, Jane, Sarah, and Claire** - for being my family away from home. I can't tell you how comforting it was to share family meals and outings with you. The genuine care and concern you showed me will always be remembered and cherished.

+ **John and Ruth** - for your sincere care for my spiritual, personal and professional well being during my time in Singapore. Your love and prayers helped to make this process more enjoyable all around.

+ **Dean, Patrick & Brandon** - for your willingness to meet up and "mentor" me on multiple levels. I will forever be grateful for the occasional "kick in the rear-end" chats that helped me to jump start this book, among other things.

+ **Armour Publishing** - for putting on a wonderful writing seminar with John Maust, which served as the real starting point for me in hearing and heeding the call to write. Especially Hong Koon, whose kind and gentle guidance took me from having ideas to writing a manuscript.

+ **Tuesday Group** - for providing rich community and fellowship that enriched my spiritual walk with God and empowered me to follow in the way He was leading. The worship, teaching, connecting and praying each week was the "soul food" that kept me strong and nourished in this writing process.

+ **Princeton "crew"** - for accepting and loving me just the way I am.

About the Author

Ali Smith grew up in Bozeman, Montana with three sisters-one of them her twin- and her parents. She left home to attend Princeton University, where she earned a Bachelor of Arts degree in Religious Studies.

After college, Ali was granted a broadcast journalism fellowship with a program called Princeton-in-Asia, which brought her to Manila, Philippines. She worked as a news anchor and reporter there for two years at the largest news network in the country. She regularly volunteered for a street children's feeding program, which eventually led to her spearheading a scholarship program for street children to go to college. She says she will always have a heart for the Philippines and is passionate about finding ways to give the children she has grown to know and love a brighter future.

Ali moved from the Philippines to Singapore, to explore more of Asia. She currently works as a news anchor and current affairs show host for Asia's premier international news network. She serves in her church's usher ministry and is a prayer leader for her young adults fellowship group. As a gifted communicator, Ali is frequently asked to speak at churches, workshops and seminars. She doesn't know how long her broadcasting career will last but her dream is to write more books and travel around the world encouraging, empowering and equipping people to live out their God-given purpose.

Ali is also a fitness buff and loves anything to do with the outdoors-especially hitting the ski slopes in the Rocky Mountains. She is also an avid runner and has run two marathons so far.

Ali Smith can be reached by email at
www.entrustingthekey.com

Also visit **www.entrustingthekey.com** for:

- ✦ more recommended reading
- ✦ dialogue and discussion with other readers
- ✦ interaction with the author
- ✦ and much more!